The Italian Legacy in The United Arab Emirates

The Italian Legacy in The United Arab Emirates: The Urban and Industrial Landscape

Edited by Lucia Pizzinato

SKIRA

Acknowledgements

This book is the result of around two years of research conducted mostly through a network, aided by the willingness of many individuals to share their time, material, backstories, and memories with me. It was a pleasure to be in contact with the various companies and architecture firms cited in this publication; my thanks go out to all of them and their representatives in Italy and the United Arab Emirates (UAE) for their concerted cooperation. I particularly benefited from the opportunity to discuss each source's work and experience in the Gulf region, specifically in the United Arab Emirates.

Identifying the various Italian companies that have a physical presence in the United Arab Emirates, as well as those that commute between Italy and UAE, has not been an easy task.

In this regard, I would like to thank two people in particular: Pasquale della Penna, widely considered the Italian "historical memory of the country," for helping me to identify the numerous Italian companies present in the United Arab Emirates; and Pasquale D'Agosto, who offered details on the various Italian architectural firms present in Abu Dhabi and Dubai.

When starting this project I consulted with friends and colleagues, who provided valuable advice and linked me to sources.

I would especially like to thank Nelida Fuccaro, Peter Hellyer, Todd Reisz, Goffredo Puccetti and Lorenzo Zoli.

I owe a considerable debt of gratitude to Francesca Bacci for her attentive listening and moral encouragement, but also concrete support with constructive comments and suggestions.

My sincere thanks to Michele Nastasi for his generosity in talking about photography with me. His photographic work and research focus on architecture and its visual implications in contemporary cities has been fundamental and inspiring.

Thank you also to the photographers Jon Wallis, Marc Goodwin (ARCHMOSPHERES), Roland Halbe, Chris Goldstrow, and Barbara Burg + Oliver Schuh (Palladium Photodesign), whose material greatly enriches the publication.

As this project was commissioned to me only a few months before the global pandemic hit and influenced our daily life, I extend immense thanks to all the Institutions, libraries, archives that publish open-access material online. Thanks to the pandemic, it would not have been be possible to consult a great many documents, journals, and papers, given the limitations of in-person consultation.

I am grateful to the New York University library, where I spent hours consulting books from its rich collection (when possible), and especially to Brad Bauer, NYUAD Head of Archives and Special Collections, for his constant availability and insight.

Thanks, are also due to the Environment Agency in Abu Dhabi, the National Library and Archives of the Ministry of Presidential Affairs and the Arabian Gulf Digital Archive.

Thank you to the contributors in the book's Expo section: Paolo Glisenti (General Commissioner for Italy at Expo 2020), Davide Rampello (Artistic Director Italian Pavilion Expo 2020), the architects Carlo Ratti and Italo Rota, LAND Architecture Studio, and Paolo Leutenegger (Duplomatic Motion Solutions).

Special thanks are also due to His Excellency Zaki Nusseibeh for writing the book's Preface.

Thank you to the Italian Ambassador Nicola Lener and the Embassy of Italy in Abu Dhabi for their trust in me in developing this project. I would acknowledge, Stefania Bonotto (Cultural Affairs Office) for her constant assistance in the journey along with this book.

Finally, a special note to the crew members of Skira Editore (Milan) for their interest, support, and dedication. Andrew Ellis (Word Studio, Milan) for his diligent efforts in correcting the various texts, and Evelina Laviano for the book's graphics.

Thank you also to Diego Radici for his immediate interest in this book.

On a personal note, thank you to my family for the constant support. And Ivan for his cooking, caring and understanding. The book is dedicated to him.

Lucia Pizzinato

Ambassador's remarks

As Ambassador of Italy to the United Arab Emirates in the year of the 50th Anniversary of the establishment of diplomatic relations between our two countries, I am very glad that my Embassy can contribute to the celebrations with this beautiful volume on Italy's architectural legacy to the UAE.

Our purpose is, in fact, to reflect on the extraordinary social and economic development that the UAE has experienced over these five decades through the lens of Italy's participation in the transformation of the country's urban and industrial landscape.

Through abundant photographic material accompanied by brief captions, this book aims to illustrate the technological and artistic features of some of the main works carried out by Italian companies and professional firms in the UAE, that are behind the intense economic and cultural bonds between our countries and our people.

The common thread in these projects is not to impose an Italian national identity on the works undertaken, but rather to discreetly and tastefully support the aspirations of the UAE to create an identity of its own in the field of architecture and urban planning. I believe that this discretion – which owes much to our natural attitude to put ourselves in the shoes of our interlocutors in order to better understand their ambitions, concerns, and hopes – is the result of the way we manage relations, be they among people, companies, or governments.

It is with the same respectful and mutually enriching approach that Italy intends to continue developing its links with the UAE, sharing its technological and organizational know-how and at the same time absorbing the constant tension to the future and innovation that is increasingly one of this country's distinctive features.

Let me finally express my deep gratitude to H.E. Zaki Nusseibeh – an honourable witness to the development of the United Arab Emirates over these decades, and a long-standing friend of Italy – for his foreword to this book, as well as to Ms Lucia Pizzinato, curator of the project, and to all the companies that contributed to its realization with their material.

H.E. Nicola Lener
Ambassador of Italy to the United Arab Emirates

Cover
The Abu Dhabi skyline from
Saadiyat Island, 2017.

Design
Marcello Francone

Editorial Coordination
Vincenza Russo

Editing
Andrew Ellis, Word Studio, Milan

Layout
Evelina Laviano

First published in Italy in 2022 by
Skira editore S.p.A.
Palazzo Casati Stampa
via Torino 61
20123 Milano
Italy
www.skira.net

Printed and bound in Italy. First edition

ISBN: 978-88-572-4712-0

Distributed in USA, Canada, Central & South America by
ARTBOOK | D.A.P. 75 Broad Street Suite 630, New York, NY 10004, USA
Distributed elsewhere in the world by Thames and Hudson Ltd., 181A High Holborn, London WC1V 7QX, United Kingdom

Contents

Preface
The Legacy of Italian Contribution to the United Arab Emirates

Zaki Anwar Nusseibeh

Cultural Advisor to H.H.
the President Chancellor
of the United Arab Emirates University

The United Arab Emirates (UAE) was born during a difficult period of turmoil across the Gulf region. At the time, most international observers doubted that the seven emirates that joined under a federal treaty possessed the military, administrative, or capital infrastructure necessary to establish a viable state.

Nevertheless, fifty years later, the UAE is now a prosperous, stable, knowledge-based society, and has an important influence on global political, economic, and cultural affairs.

The remarkable development and success of the country is the culminating legacy of wise, visionary, courageous, and tenacious leadership by its founders, coupled with the ideas, advice, and investments of a multiplicity of partners from around the globe.

Those partners include an impressive number of Italian architects, businessmen, companies, and individuals who played a significant role in supporting the success story of the UAE. Those involved are of course multinational giants, such as the Italian state carbohydrate industries ENI and Saipem. But they also comprised many gifted Italian individuals and smaller companies in the construction and design sector, who made the UAE their second home.

My earliest recollection of an Italian luxury product in Abu Dhabi concerns a set of exquisite Murano glass chandeliers hanging in one of Abu Dhabi's first stately homes, known as the Mushrif Palace.

Built by the late Sheikh Hamdan bin Mohammed Al Nahyan as a private residence in the early 1970s, the edifice soon passed into public domain to become the first official guest palace to receive visiting heads of state and dignitaries including the king of Jordan, and the late King Hussein. The original palace was eventually demolished and a newer version built in its place; this served as the official state palace for several years until it was superseded by the construction of Qasr Al Watan, which was inaugurated in 2015.

Of course, modern-day visitors to the Sheikh Zayed Grand Mosque continue to be stunned by its grand design. The mosque was constructed between 1996 and 2007 in a joint venture between Italian contractors Salini-Impregilo (now Webuild) and Rizzani de Eccher, together with other Italian and international partners. Its expansive ornamental marble floors designed and laid by the Italian flooring contractors Fantini Mosaici is considered to be the largest example of marble mosaic in the world, and comprises exquisite stone quarried in Italy's northern Alto Adige region (Südtirol).

This journey from those first Murano glass artefacts of the early 1970s, to the Italian marble and Italian design today, testifies to a long and extraordinary partnership between the UAE and Italy, a strategic bond of expanding horizons of cooperation that mirrored the remarkable transition of the Emirates from the early 1970s into the twenty-first century.

This is because the history of the UAE witnessed the transformation of the social, technical, urban, and industrial landscape at a speed and scale that has few precedents. The country's physical infrastructure serves as evidence of the directions and phases of this trajectory, and the contributions of the finest international partners.

Italian architects, designers, and contractors continue to number among its most important collaborators.

The mutually advantageous strategic partnership between Italy and the UAE in this domain continues to thrive today. The future of the UAE lies in its ability to foster and harness the creativity and energies of what has become a vibrant, harmonious, and interconnected multicultural society. Its vision is to be a global leader in sustainable social, political, economic, and environmental development. It goes without saying that the UAE cannot succeed in this ambition in isolation: through its own efforts, it must serve and invigorate the wellbeing of the nation and the region, but also the global community. It must pursue policies that attract and welcome the interests of all nations and their people.

Diplomatic relations between Italy and the UAE began in 1971. Italy established its embassy in Abu Dhabi in 1979, and the UAE established its own in the Italian capital of Rome in 1981, with a new headquarters built in 2017. To the delight of the UAE, in 2021 Italy inaugurated the Italian Cultural Institute in Abu Dhabi, which acts as a driving force for initiatives and projects of cultural cooperation between the two nations. Moreover, it is an integral part of the diplomatic network of Italy's Ministry of Foreign Affairs, and the first Italian Cultural Institute participating so far in the Gulf Cooperation Council (GCC).

Relations between the UAE and Italy are based on solid foundations of shared visions and interests in political, economic, and cultural fields. We have exchanged our resources to energize a process of dynamic, creative, and mutually beneficial development. The UAE and Italy share synergies in tourism, retail, and manufacturing. Both are significant business and logistics hubs within their respective regions that have diversified their economies in recent years. Today, the UAE is Italy's principal commercial partner in the Middle East and North Africa, and to date over 12,000 Italian start-ups operate here, generating a throughput worth over 700 million ($846,000).

Italy enjoys a longstanding global reputation for culture, artistry, agricultural production, manufacturing skill, automotive engineering, sporting endeavours, and tireless pursuit of the finest distinction. One might say that the history of the entire world bears the hallmarks of the country's valiant and intrepid citizens, in all fields.

The UAE's contribution to Expo Milan 2015 introduced the planning principles of the traditional desert town: the pavilion's interior of shaded streets evoked the experience of the UAE's early communities, while demonstrating the natural energy efficiency of their compact urban form. Influenced by ancient urban layouts, the paths through the pavilion were suggestive of the narrow pedestrian streets and courtyards of the classic desert township – and its contemporary reinterpretation in the sustainable Masdar City masterplan in Abu Dhabi.

Therefore, it is no surprise that Italy has left its mark in the United Arab Emirates, nor that the Italian pavilion at the Expo 2020 Dubai has been launched under the theme, "Beauty Connects People". The architecture of the pavilion presents to the world the renowned multidisciplinary skills, talents, and ingenuity of the Italian people, and the desire to apply these resources to foster international connections. No doubt, the pavilion will engender the cooperation and innovation that today's global sustainability demands.

CRA–Carlo Ratti Associati and Italo Rota
Office Building, Italian Pavilion, Dubai EXPO, 2021.
The Italian Pavilion's motto "Beauty connects people" lights up at night on the building's curtain façade made of nautical rope of recycled plastic with incorporated LED lights that transform the entire surface into a multimedia surface.

Introduction

Lucia Pizzinato

Over the past fifty years, the United Arab Emirates has undergone a remarkable and completely unprecedented transformation: from being largely known for its fishing, pearl diving, and trade villages, to each emirate becoming recognized as international city with its own distinct characteristics, shaped by the direct involvement of their respective rulers. The country has undergone a rapid transformation and expansion from the nomadic origins and desert terrain to an multi-urban entity fuelled by the wealth generated from the discovery of rich oil reserves back in 1958.

In this context, oil emerged as "the protagonist and social and cultural catalyst" that shaped the rising global metropolis.[1] The income generated from the underground reserves enabled each emirate to develop large-scale urban projects designed to attract trade and foreign investment that contributed to the rapid growth of the cities. Aware that region's oil resources were vast but nonetheless limited, the UAE invested strategically in an economy of diversification. This diversified economy is based mainly on "tourism, investment in alternative energy, infrastructure, and technology, trade, real estate sector",[2] and finds its manifestation in the construction of megaprojects and through the cities' multicultural nature and "flow".[3]

In the last twenty years, the cities of Dubai and Abu Dhabi have scaled up in urban development reflecting an interplay of international influences with a "local vernacular". International architects, engineers and builders – many coming from Italy – have grown their network on the global crossroads of the UAE; a place where ideas, people, and cultures meet.

This book presents the seminal findings of an ongoing initiative to document the history of the contribution of the Italian construction companies and architecture firms in shaping the urban and industrial landscape of the United Arab Emirates.

I have highlighted the Italian contribution with a close analysis of the main architectural projects that have a particular resonance in the region, and are designed by Italian architecture studios and built by reputable Italian construction firms and companies.

However, instead of simply celebrating and having generic discussions about the extraordinary buildings in the Emirates, we look at the developments and various contributions that Italian companies give to the region, establishing a prosperous relationship built on a constant dialogue with their expertise and trust. Therefore, the aim is to investigate the bond between Italy and the UAE, and the value determined by the Italian expertise within an expanding urban context.

Within a chronological evolution through construction and architecture, each section of the book explores the Italian contribution to shaping the landscapes of the newly established federation in 1971 and its emergence on a global scale. This unfolding chronology takes the reader on a journey from the years that forerun the official unification to the present day, including the UAE's Golden Jubilee, and Expo 2020 Dubai – the first International Exhibition in the MENASA (Middle East, North Africa, South Asia) region.

The following questions are addressed in order to provide answers that reflect the Italian legacy in the United Arab Emirates. How did Italian companies contribute to shaping the urban and industrial landscape of the country? What projects have been developed? What are their contributions to the landmarks that characterize the country? Moreover, which other lesser-known projects are significant to this study. For what periods is it possible to trace the presence of Italians in the area?

To do so means emplacing the various companies in the history of the United Arab Emirates and the current time in which they play a significant role.

The majority of the forty-six projects presented in this book are from the emirates Abu Dhabi, Dubai, and Sharjah respectively. However, there are many other interesting projects developed in the country by Italian firms which for reasons of privacy committments have not been included.

The main projects developed by Italians are collected through detailed descriptive pages in the two main sections that characterize the book: the urban and industrial landscape.

The urban landscape section focuses on the transformation of the cities from the early development until the emergence of advanced urbanism characterized by the proliferation of spectacular architecture and mega-scale infrastructures such as skyscrapers, bridges, transportation hubs, roads, waterfront developments, malls, and entertainment venues. In these scenarios, modern architecture has embedded traditional motifs from the Arab culture and its heritage, aiming to create – and at the same time preserve – a distinctive local identity "in the face of global homogenization".[4]

Meanwhile, the industrial landscape section focuses on the productive and energy sector of the UAE, which is concentrated in remote areas such as Jebel Dhanna, Ruwais, or Mussafah in Abu Dhabi and the port town of Jebel Ali – located southwest of Dubai. It is also part of the UAE's diversified economy plan that aims to "empower industrial growth by promoting the adoption of advanced technology and enhancing its role in stimulating the national economy".[5]

The pattern of the industrial landscape consists of infrastructures secluded and secured in the vast desert area. Here, sculptural drill sites, jackup rigs, night flares from the vents are spread across the desert dunes, along the shore, or out at sea. Elements such as mining castles, rigs for oil extraction, pipelines with their essential linearity define this landscape. And recalling Rania Gosn and El Hadi Jazairy's words, oil infrastructure "fixating itself in space materializes a territory" and "shapes geography".[6]

These two landscapes – industrial and urban – are intertwined, since both flourish through the exploitation of the natural resources of oil and gas present in the soil.

Research Methodology

To produce the research presented in this book, especially bringing to light the very early project of the new-born federation, a constant dialogue with people from various companies was fundamental. Through word-of-mouth and those willing to share more about their work and their experience in the UAE, I was able to build a network that helped me to reach out to professionals working in Italian companies or architecture studios that the UAE had called in to contribute to the early development of the cities.

Through these connections I gained access to some preserved documents, journals of the developments they contributed to, and photos. Furthermore, valuable materials – tangible photographs and intangible memories – enabled me to track a putative timeline for the Italian presence in the UAE through architecture and industrial projects, from 1971 up until today. One might expect that modernization – precisely its capacity to calibrate and record – would leave behind an archive of some kind. Unfortunately, this is not the case. Gathering material and documents was quite a challenge, heightened by the fact that the book's research started in February 2020, a month before the entire world was shut down by the global pandemic. Considering the circumstances, relying on digital archives and open access material was even more critical than ever.

An invaluable fund of information for this book was provided by the online archive of the Arabian Gulf Digital Archives (AGDA), property of the National Library and Archives of the United Arab Emirates (NLA) and in collaboration with The National Archives (TNA) of the United Kingdom. This archive is a collection of historical documents comprising extensive correspondence, agreements, letters between leading players, officials, and governments, providing a detailed history of the Arabian Gulf states. The material consulted includes records of the British Foreign Office (FO) and Foreign and Commonwealth Office (FCO), correspondence of the British Political Agents in Dubai and Abu Dhabi with the Political Residents in Bahrain.

Additionally, I consulted a wide range of documentary sources related to architecture, press material, and reviews, websites of the firms themselves and the public administration, journals, local newspapers, general magazines, articles dedicated to construction, architecture, engineering, and assorted non-specialized literature.

I am sure that there are more untold stories to discover. This book is not intended to be a comprehensive research of the UAE's evolution, but rather an insightful documentation of the Italian contribution to the urban and industrial development of the country's distinct landscape. I therefore invite anyone who wishes to share their story and experience in the region to contact me.

A Discourse on Photography

The book unfolds on two different levels. With the descriptions of the various selected projects comprising the two sections – the urban and the industrial landscape – the first level is an exploration of the contribution and expertise of the different Italian companies in realizing the various architectural projects thanks to their technology-engineering expertise and innovative approach.

The second level is photography, which is an essential part of this research, as it works not only as documentation and representation of the architecture per se, but also reveals and reflects on the urban landscape as a dynamic place in transformation and evolution.

Collecting and researching photographs in order to convey this idea of an evolving urban place was quite a challenge as I found myself involved in a discourse related to photography and the representation of the Gulf cities that was impossible to ignore.

Someone may take for granted that photographing a completed project is fairly usual for a company or architecture firm, or that it is quite easy to find photos of well-recognized architecture considering the high circulation of images of the Gulf cities (particularly Abu Dhabi and Dubai) and their landmarks. Again, this is not the case, and the reason is twofold. Firstly, nowadays, it seems there is no need to photograph architecture in a time when renderings – computer-generated images – are so photorealistic and accurate that it is difficult to distinguish them from an actual photograph. The second reason regards the circulation of images and how they are depicted.

Since its inception, the photographic medium has had a particular resonance in exploring and representing architecture. As stated by Andrew Higgott and Timothy Wray: "photography is fundamental in shaping our understanding of the city and in urban design practices" [...] "the photograph is not a simple representation of an external reality but constructs its own meaning and reconstructs its subject."[7] Thus, photography plays an important role in constructing an image that contributes to the transformation and framing of the public perception of a specific place.[8]

In the era of globalization, cities invest in their "iconic" image through spectacular architectures that display features largely shared between cities, creating "global urban imaginary" as the skyline that is familiar to everyone. This tendency highlights how images – especially today with the introduction of architectural rendering create an idealized image – affect the urban transformation, and how it is perceived by the broader public.[9]

For these reasons, the photographic image influences the urban transformation process at various levels. From the more specialized ones who design, create, build, to a more general group such as the public, whose consensus is crucial in deciding the success of a particular architecture or urban development, a concept that is well explained by Ponzini and Nastasi.[10]

In this process, photography affects the way we see since we are all used to certain types of architecture, which brings fulfilment by being photographed continuously by visitors, tourists, etc.[11]

Important in photographing today's cities with their architecture is to find the correct balance between the peculiarity of each place because all cities are different, even if they seem to resemble one another.[12] In urbanistic terms, they are not the same. In terms of visual representation, it means keeping the distance from the conventional rules of architectural photography, where the subject – the building – is photographed as a pure object without any context. People are not present except to simply work as a spatial measure. All these elements convey an idea of abstraction that neglects the complexity of the contemporary urban landscapes "facilitating the spectacle". [13]

This tendency has been particularly evident in the representation of the Gulf cities over the recent years, where architectural projects have been mainly represented towards rendering and photographed on a "clean slate" with neither context nor references – known as *tabula rasa*.[14]

The context made of elements usually left out of the frame – sands, concrete, the skeleton of upcoming construction, people – are essential elements that define the urban fabric.[15] Considering these aspects, the group of photos selected for the book not only depict the building and city infrastructures presented. It aims to offer open circumstances that allow the eyes to move around the image, highlighting the photo's peripheral areas, whose distinctive elements visually convey the fleeting and the complexity of different urban spaces, architectural forms, and temporality.

Following pages: The Abu Dhabi skyline from Saadiyat Island, 2017.

[1] M. Vali, *Crude* (exhibition catalogue) (United Arab Emirates: Art Jameel, 2018), p.10.
[2] M. Al Asoomi (2 December 2015), "How diversification drives the UAE economy", *Gulf News:* https://gulfnews.com/business/analysis/how-diversification-drives-the-uae-economy-1.1630352 (accessed 20 December 2021).
[3] This reflects Manuel Castellas's concept of urban reality as a "space of flows", by which he defines space as a network of flux involving people, goods, information, and capital. Mina Akhavan in *Gateway: Revisiting Dubai as a Port City,* references Castellas with regard to Dubai's diversify economy: M. Akhavan, "Gateway: Revisiting Dubai as a Port City", in *The New Arab Urban: Gulf Cities of Wealth, Ambition, and Distress*, edited by H. Molotch and D. Ponzini (NYU Press, 2019), pp. 175–193.
[4] A. Andraos, N. Akawi, and C. Blanchfield (eds.), *The Arab City: Architecture and Representation* (Columbia Books on Architecture and the City, 2016), pp. 7–17.
[5] www.moiat.gov.ae/en/about-us/about-the-strategy.
[6] Design Earth (Rania Ghosn and El Hadi Jazairy), "Geography and oil: The Territory of Externalities," in *Infrastructure Space*, edited by Andreas Ruby and Ilka Ruby (Berlin: Ruby Press, 2017), pp. 361–366.
[7] A. Higgott and T. Wray, *Camera Constructs: Photography, Architecture and the Modern City* (Routledge, 2016), pp. 51–61.
[8] C. Lindner and M. Meissner (eds.), *The Routledge Companion to Urban Imaginaries* (Routledge, 2019).
[9] Another imaginary so common, is the waterfront development. To know more about the various critics around renderings, please see M. Nastasi "The City of Renderings. Photorealism, spectacle and abstraction in contemporary urban landscapes", in R.A. Alcolea, and J. Tárrago-Mingo (eds.), Congreso internacional: Inter photo arch "Interacciones", celebrado en Pamplona, los días 2 al 4 de Noviembre de 2016, pp. 274–285.
[10] D. Ponzini and M. Nastasi, "Toward a photographic urbanism? Images iconizing cities and swaying urban transformation", in *The Routledge Companion to Urban Imaginaries*, edited by C. Lindner and M. Meissner (Routledge, 2019), pp. 217–231.
[11] Ibid.
[12] The discourse of the similarities between cities has been investigated by D. Ponzini and M. Nastasi in *Starchitecture: Scenes, Actors and Spectacles in Contemporary Cities* (2nd ed., New York: The Monacelli Press, 2016).
[13] The conventions of architectural representation are widely discussed by Michele Nastasi in "A Gulf of Images: Photography and the Circulation of Spectacular Architecture", in *The New Arab Urban: Gulf Cities of Wealth, Ambition, and Distress*, edited by H. Molotch and D. Ponzini (NYU Press, 2019), pp. 99–129.
[14] H. Molotch and D. Ponzini (eds.), *The New Arab Urban: Gulf Cities of Wealth, Ambition, and Distress* (NYU Press, 2019).
[15] These aspects have also been discussed in a conversation between myself and Michele Nastasi in the online event organized by the Italian Cultural Institute in Abu Dhabi, held in June 2021, regarding the recent publication of Nastasi's photobook *Arabian Transfer* (Hatje Canz Verlag, 2021).

A History of Italian Companies in the United Arab Emirates

Lucia Pizzinato

An early presence

Italian presence in the Islamic World

Since Antiquity, the Arabian Gulf has been a place of interest for many cultures, as it was the centre of most of the routes between India and the Mediterranean Sea. Well known is the presence of Portuguese, Dutch, and British in the Arab Peninsula.[1] However, over the centuries the Italians were variously involved along the coast of the Arab Gulf and especially in the wider Islamic world.

The presence of the Italians in the Arabian Gulf dates back to the sixteenth century, when merchants – especially Venetians – explored the sea route to India discovered by the Portuguese around 1497–1499.[2] The primary reason of their presence was for commercial interests, in order to establish a business exchange centre, particularly to and from the Indian subcontinent. Thus, try to restore their power and trade position as they were before in the East. Indeed, Venice had played a leading role in commercial maritime activities as "the Venetians were the sole corporate link between Europe and the Arab regions until the end of the fifteenth century".[3]

Among those who ventured into exploration in the Far East areas were Italian missionaries, merchants, scholars, and travellers whose journals have greatly contributed to our knowledge of the Arabian Peninsula and the Indies.[4]

Gasparo Balbi, "Viaggio delle Indie Orientali (1579–1588)"

Noteworthy are the adventures of a Venetian jeweller and gem merchant Gasparo Balbi (born ca. 1550, Venice),[5] who began a long journey to India and the Far East, searching for pearling sites in 1579. In his travel journal titled *Viaggio delle Indie Orientali*, Balbi recorded his nine-year voyage (1579–1588) with important information about the Arabian Peninsula in this early period.

During his journey, in Chapter *XIIII* of his diary he noted down the names of various territories of the eastern part of the Arabian coast of the Gulf he visited, where pearls were in abundance.[6]

The names of places listed are effectively the first record of what would later become the United Arab Emirates territories: "Daas (Das), Emegorcenon (Qarnein), Anzevi (Azanah), Zerecho (Zirkuh), Delmephialmas (Dalma), Sirbeniast (Sir Bani Yas), Aldane (Dhanna), Cherizan (identified as Khor Qirqishan, just off Abu Dhabi island), Dibei (Dubai), Sarba (Sharjah), Agimen (Ajman), Emegivien (Un al-Qaiwain), Rasalchime (Ra's al Khaimah), Sircorcor (Khor al-Khuwair), Debe (Dibba), Chorf (Khor Fakkan) and Chelb (Kalba)".[7]

This Italian diary is quite remarkable, since "practically none of the names of places on the coast between Qatar and Ras Al Khaimah occur in other sources before the end of the eighteenth century [...]", as Jons Slot states.[8] Thus, the book basically offers the first printed mention of the Bani Yas Island.[9] From this island originates the Bani Yas tribal confederation,[10] from which the Al Nahyan and Al Maktoum dynasties descend, the ruling families of today's Abu Dhabi and Dubai, respectively.[11] It is not a coincidence that a copy of the book is part of His Highness Sheikh Khaled bin Mohammed bin Zayed Al Nahyan's collection, and is exhibited at Qasr Al Watan – the Presidential Palace – in the room titled "House of Knowledge".

Tribal confederation and Trucial States

The seven independent sheikhdoms (Abu Dhabi, Dubai, Sharjah, Ajman, Umm al Quwain, Fujairah, Ras Al Khaimah) were represented by the respective ruling families. They became a British protectorate in 1853 and under the name of Trucial States until their unification in 1971.[12]

From pearls to oil, towards unification

From the late nineteenth century through to the second decade of the twentieth, pearl diving was an essential source for the economy of the Trucial States, along with other marine activities such as fishing.[13] The shallow blue waters of the Arab Gulf and its neighbouring islands were, indeed, a rich place for pearling beds. With the increasing international demand for pearls, traders arrived along the shore to purchase pearls for their European clients.[14]

The introduction of cultivated pearls in 1930 in Japan led to the decline of the pearl industry, and this ran parallel with the worldwide depression followed by World War II, leaving the population to find a new source of economic revival.[15] In this scenario, the British government's intervention was vital to provide supplies to sustain the sheikdoms.[16] However, a new wealth was going to be found under the seabed in the form of oil and gas. From there, the industrial and urban development of the entire region began, marked by the withdrawal of the conservative Sheikh Shakhbout bin Sultan Al Nahyan in favour of his brother the visionary Sheikh Zayed bin Sultan Al Nahyan, in 1966. And then with the Unification of the sheikdoms and the formation of the United Arab Emirates on 2 December 1971 by the hand of Sheik Zayed, who became the President of the newly formed Federation.

Italian companies shaping the urban landscape.

The United Arab Emirates are well known for their rapid urban development and investment in extraordinary projects, due to the prosperity generated from gas and oil revenue.

Their architecture and worldwide exposure have been at the forefront since the mid-2000s. Everything that happened before seems ignored, with the misconception of a country risen without context and lacking in history.[17] Instead, the Emirates bring a complex story related to their developments and formation, with each emirate having its distinctions in terms of architectural development, urban setting, and history. During the Trucial States (1856–1971), the British government had a substantial influence on the sheikdoms, handling their external affairs through the establishment of Political Agents in Sharjah, Dubai, and Abu Dhabi.[18]

Dispelling the commonplace

Following the discovery of oil reserves in 1966, a mutual agreement between the British government and the ruling families of the Trucial States opened the field to foreign companies, architects, and engineers, with the aim of pushing the development of the region.

Transport network development

Since 1960 the primary developments regarded mainly the transport infrastructure. In order to facilitate the exchange of goods among the local markets and interregional activities, the ancient caravan routes of the Bedouin and tracks of compacted sand connecting the major villages were converted into paved roads, creating unity among the settlements.[19]

Among the companies involved in such development, there were Italian construction firms engaged in the Gulf region.

One of them is the Italian firm Zompi. At that time in Aden (Yemen), while working for the British government, the firm was consulted by Sheikh Zayed for the creation of a concrete airstrip in Buraimi in July 1963.[20] Even though the tender did not reach the final stage, the company carried out other works.[21] As mentioned by *The Gulf* newspaper in an interview with one of the Italian company's employees, Giovanni Cantalupo, the company developed the first roads between Al Shindagha to Zabeel and near Al Maktoum bridge and the main arterial road in Dubai, at the request of Shaikh Rashid bin Saeed Al Maktoum.[22]

In 1966 one of the most significant infrastructure projects took place: the first paved highway built to bind the Trucial States.[23] The 116 kilometres of road connecting Sharjah to Ras Al Khaimah[24] was appointed to the Italian consulting firm Sauti.[25] Today that road, completed in 1972, is part of the E 11 highway.

The emerging of a modern city

The merger of the sheikhdoms and the establishment of the federation of the United Arab Emirates, following the expiration of the British Treaty in 1971[26] and the nomination of Sheikh Zayed as president, prompted the country to start an unprecedented social improvement and advancement, as well as the emergence of a modern city.

Diplomatic relations between Italy and UAE

The same year of the unification, Italy and the UAE established their bilateral and diplomatic relations based on shared vision and interests.[27] A unanimous willingness to combine forces was noted during the visit of the UAE Minister of Foreign Affairs in Rome, by invitation of the Italian Economic Minister in 1974.[28]

In 1978 a visit of the Italian Economic Minister in Abu Dhabi strengthened the relationship between the two countries, and extended the mutual collaboration with the direct participation of Italian companies on the territory.[29]

Several Italian firms were already present, mainly in the capital of Abu Dhabi, as one can see from the Timeline reconstruction (page 34).

With their expertise, they helped to develop projects that are the fruit of Sheikh Zayed's vision of the growth and progress of the country.

Zayed Vision of nation building

The founding father of the UAE shaped the country's evolution and "channelled large sums of investment into the culture and building infrastructure while also embracing globalization to modify cultural traditions in a non-threatening way and share the newly found wealth with the native society."[30] Development in transportation, healthcare facilities, educational institutions, and environmentalism were incentivized, playing a crucial role in nation-building.[31]

Environment and agriculture

The first focus of Zayed's vision was on the environment and natural ecosystem preservation.

Zayed's environmental philosophy aimed to curb desertification, making the desert a green land, and creating a self-sufficient agricultural production.[32] In order to achieve this, he started an afforestation programme and invited the world's leading horticulturist and landscaping experts to plant trees in the desert and develop agriculture. Among them was the Italian company Sgaravatti Group, which in its 200 years of history had developed the idea of the perfect garden and revolutionized the history of European horticulture.[33]

With a contract signed in 1977, Sgaravatti Group create several plant nurseries with innovative irrigation systems and contributed to the realization of Zayed's extraordinary green legacy.

As Zayed's words recall, "they used to say that agriculture has no future [in the UAE]. But with God's blessing and our determination, we have succeeded in transforming the desert into a green land".[34] By 1990 new fewer than 130 million trees were planted across the Abu Dhabi emirate.[35]

Connecting the hinterland

The next stage of development was expanding the transport network to incentivize the connection in the hinterland. Italy's Italconsult, an engineering firm, drew the main road connecting Abu Dhabi and Al Ain. Soon others followed in the western region of Abu Dhabi, as the design and construction of both the Madinat Zayed to Ghayathi Road and the improvement of Al Ain internal road network were completed in 2015.[36]

Healthcare

The expansion of the transport sector entailed the development of further infrastructures such as hospitals. The Mafraq Hospital was designed for the purpose of granting the presence of a first-class medical facilities within the radius of 30 kilometres from the new Abu Dhabi airports. Assigned to the British consultant firm Sir Alexander Gibb & Partners, the hospital project was awarded to the Italian firms General Planning and built in-place by FEAL S.p.A. When it opened in 1983,[37] it was a cutting-edge hospital equipped with the most modern medical machinery for treatment and diagnostic purposes, "operating according to the highest world standards".[38]

Reform and transition

In Abu Dhabi, the Italian construction company FEAL also contributed to the façade construction of the modernist architecture of Le Meridien Hotel, situated in the Tourist Club Area; it was "the second international hotel to open in the capital after the Hilton".[39]

In the 1990s, under the specific enlightened vision based on moderation and religious

Culture of tolerance and cooperation over diversity

tolerance in UAE, the Sheikh Zayed Grand Mosque was planned.[40]

Architectural expression of "the past and the present" of the Islamic tradition, the project and construction of the iconic landmark saw the participation of worldwide expertise, among which several Italian companies. The cooperation between the international firms in the mosque realization could be interpreted as a manifestation of the unity between the cultures, regardless of difference, an essential value of Sheikh Zayed's legacy.[41]

The external envelope was constructed by

A booming economy: megaprojects and starchitecture

Salini Impregilo (now Webuild) and Rizzani de Eccher, while BMS Progetti, a multidisciplinary design firm, developed the dome's design.

The interior design of the Grand Mosque is by the Italian architecture firm SPATIUM – Lorenzo Carmellini and Rocco Magnoli. The floral decoration in marble and precious stones is handmade by Fantini Mosaici, an expression of high craftsmanship. For the mosaics' realization,

Italian artisan tradition and craftsmanship

Fantini Mosaici opened its international workshop in Mussafah, where the company, to this day, creates unique and unrepeatable artworks embedding tradition (traditional artisanal techniques) and innovation (state-of-the-art technology) – both symbols of excellence and ambassador for Italian craftsmanship at the international level. The work done for the mosque opened new opportunities for Fantini Mosaici. To the company was then commissioned the majestic Presidential Palace, the domes of the almost complete Sheikh Khalifa bin Zayed Al Nahyan Mosque in Al Ain, and the interiors of shops of luxury brands. With the architecture firm SPATIUM is also the realization of Palazzo Versace in Dubai.

All the Italian companies mentioned above will continue to have significant involvement in remarkable projects in the UAE in the coming years, establishing a long-lasting relationship with the country.

With Zayed's death in 2004, and the succession to the presidency of his son Sheikh Khalifa bin Zayed Al Nahyan (2004–2022) – named Crown Prince of Abu Dhabi – the government underwent restructuring. This corresponded to several changes in the urban asset regulations, property laws, and the rise of real-estate development companies.

The changes impacted the development of the city's urban form and growth, resulting in a construction boom and further transformation. The model adopted by Abu Dhabi was quite similar to the one used in Dubai, especially regarding the real-estate strategies and the emergence of ambitious plans, although the differences between the two cities are often remarked upon.[42]

Since the 1980s Dubai has based itself as a centre for "regional and global trade activity", and took the strategic decision to invest heavily in the high-tech industry and spectacular mega-projects, in order to emerge as a hub for tourism, leisure, and entertainment, as a means of balancing its dwindling oil reserves. Tourism became the key element around which the city evolved in order to diversify its economy.[43]

Significant investment has been made in the hotel industry (e.g., Burji Khalifa, Burji Al Arab), reclaimed islands (the Palm, the World), the completion of the airport and transport facilities, to create an image of the city based on progress and dynamism, consolidated through iconic architecture and place branding.[44]

Under the presidency of Sheikh Zayed, Abu Dhabi has emerged as a thoroughly modern city, and hence established as the capital of the UAE, with the new government. Furthermore, the intent was to transform the city into a global player with tourism, culture, education as the main economic driver. Key developments such as Al

Maryah Island, Al Raha Beach, Yas Island, the Saadiyat Cultural District, the new sustainable urban development of Masdar City were conceived as core features, setting a new standard for the city's advancement. With the formation of the Urban Structure Framework Plan and the vision 2030 that delineates the city's current and future development plan as a guiding principle of future transformation, Abu Dhabi's goal was set to be "a contemporary expression of an Arab city [...]" and its "urban fabric and community infrastructure will enable the values, social arrangements, culture and mores of this Arab community."[45]

"In 2007, the UAE drew the highest number of new investment projects in the region, rising from 88 in 2002 to 282 in 2006, with total Foreign Direct Investment (FDI) in the country valued at Dh70 billion (US$ 19 billion). This figure had increased to around Dh75 billion (US$ 20.4 billion) in 2007. The UAE ranked 37 globally on the Davos World Competitiveness Index for 2007/08 and first on the Arab World Competitiveness Index."[46]

New contracting architecture companies and engineering consultants were invited onboard for their expertise and experience in tall buildings, particularly western companies, as they were considered as synonymous of professionalism.[47] Moreover, foreign companies were facilitated to establish a branch in the region, thanks to the expansion of free zones. The country has seen the rise of mega-development and "starchitecture" in a vast desertscape, a spectacle for economic and political aims.[48] A new urban and spatial perception of the desert that marks the early twenty-first century attracted the attention of the international media.

Cutting-edge projects pushing the boundaries of existing technology require the intervention of advanced know-how for their construction, as they have to face the severity of the climate and the peculiarity of the region's topography.

The increase of work opportunities in the United Arab Emirates attracted various Italian companies that accelerated their participation in the international context and opened a branch in the region. As reported by the Italian newspaper *Il Sole 24 Ore*: "The commissions acquired by the Italian companies between July 2006 and January 2008 were four billions and 492 million euros, while from 2002 to June 2006, four billions and 990 million US dollars."[49]

Many projects have seen the interventions of renowned Italian companies in the construction and manufacturing sectors, nurturing an ever-growing appreciation and affection towards Italian design and production expertise.

Italian avant-garde in construction and manufacturing of advanced architecture

In this period of high-rise buildings, distinguished for their aesthetics, height, and shape, constructability became essential in realizing these advanced architectures.

Established in the Arabian Gulf since 1973, with its office in Dubai, Swissboring Overseas Piling Corporation (part of the Italy's Trevi Group) has applied its specialized expertise to about 5,000 soil investigations underpinning and grouting projects, and over 1,300 piling/shoring projects in the United Arab Emirates. Several soaring towers of the Dubai skyline have foundations made by this company, such as the Index Tower, Marina Gate, and ICD Brookfield. In Abu Dhabi, iconic structures such as the Ferrari World, or the areas of Al Raha Beach and Al Sowa Island today known as Al Maryah Island, new urban developments of commercial, residential and retail components.

The structural system of curtain-wall façades used in tall buildings represented a novel challenge to satisfy the requirements of the new projects designed by architects inclined to use high-tech design forms. Permasteelisa Group, acclaimed for realizing visionary challenging architectural projects worldwide that combine art and science, developed site-specific state-of-the-art technology able to satisfy the most demanding requests in realizing façades and envelopes of high complexity. Among the featured projects developed in the Gulf is the Bukathir in Sharjah and the state-of-the-art Coca-Cola Arena, the latest designed by Populous. Of particular note is the challenging circular architecture of the Aldar Headquarters, in which Permasteelisa Group built the façade in collaboration with the Italian firm Metra, which produces high-quality decorative elements in aluminium.

The expression of high Italian manufacture is also featured in the world's tallest tower, the Burji Khalifa, completed in 2008. Meanwhile the

Prysmian Group – "energy leader and telecom cable system manufacturer"[50] – participated in the planning of the advanced wiring systems for the building's elevators, supplying the tower's electrical circuits and overseeing the complex fire safety systems and the performance specifications of the elevators.

The same year of completion of the Burji Khalifa, the global financial crisis brought a temporary halt in the country's development, with various projects put on hold or delayed. However, despite the serious setbacks, the public sectors saw more transparency and greater awareness of the city's growth.[51]

Outlook

Change of direction: preserving the urban fabric

One significant development was the shift of attention toward environment factors and the recognition of the need to adopt sustainability measures in all further development and construction, along with a new focus on alternative energy, and greater emphasis on the preservation of Arabic heritage by adopting historical architectural forms that evoke tradition, rather than indulge in spectacular modern ones for the sake of it.

With this change of direction, the ambitious plans continued, but were more regulated and in a "manner that is far more quality and focused on the future inhabitants".[52]

In this context, Italian professionals, architects, and engineers found fertile terrain to develop projects that stand out for their distinction, creativity, and sustainability, bringing an added value that lies in the qualitative choice of the materials, artisanal attention to detail, and research in innovative solutions that are environmentally responsive.

Discovery of oil reserves, and foreign oil concession

Performative urbanism: Italian creativity, sustainability and innovation

Among those brought in were such firms specialized in architecture and interior design as M+N Architecture, iBridge Engineering Consultancy in collaboration with Studio Cotefa, Whitespace Architects – UPA Consultancy & UPA Italia, MMA Projects, Studio Costa Architecture, De8_Architetti and, ACPV Architects Antonio Citterio and Patricia Viel. In each case, these firms delivered an extensive range of high-quality projects related to the needs of the various sectors, including educational, hospitality, healthcare, residential, and commercial. Furthermore, highly specialized Italian companies whose work is based on the strong synergy with renowned architects took part in a remarkable programme of architectural realizations.

A significant example is the Louvre Museum in Abu Dhabi, rising from the water of the Saadiyat Island Cultural District, a place assigned to host world-class museums.

The extraordinary Louvre Abu Dhabi is the result of the symbiotic encounter of diverse expertise. Several Italian companies collaborated with the French architect Jean Nouvel to complete the marvellous museum.

In its fifty years of growth and progress from a small desert country, the UAE has become a nation of global standing.

The union has achieved a great many important targets in various sectors, with an impressive economic and urban evolution spanning a mere five decades. An accomplishment reached through its leadership and openness to other cultures, welcoming world-wide expertise and talents, many of whom of Italian origin, sharing ideas and creativity for the common aim to develop a country of global status.

These features are also essential for the following comprehensive development plan for the next fifty years of the UAE.[53]

Italian companies shaping the industrial landscape.

In 1930 oil exploration started in the region; nevertheless, in 1958 oil was discovered near Das Island at Umm Shaif, northwest of the Abu Dhabi mainland, and since then the site has developed into a significant oil installation.[54]

The discovery of oil reserves attracted the interest of the major western oil companies in the area. However, because of the strict control exerted by the British, at first any foreign intervention along the Gulf Coast was excluded, and it was not until later in 1965, when the British relaxed control over the Trucial Coast – and withdrew in 1971 – that foreign companies were allowed to solicit oil concessions.[55]

Among the oil companies presenting their offer for a new land concession in Abu Dhabi was the Azienda Generale Italiana Petroli (AGIP),[56] in a consortium with Phillips Petroleum Company and American Independent Oil Co. (Amin Oil), as is reported in a letter dated 21 May 1966 from the British Political Agent.[57]

One year later, Phillips, Aminoil, and AGIP jointly obtained the concession (with each company taking a one-third share): on 21 January 1967 the official concession agreement with Abu Dhabi's ruler Sheikh Zayed was signed, for the exploration and exploitation of petroleum in four onshore areas relinquished by the Abu Dhabi Petroleum Company (ADPC).[58] The agreement drawn up in "modern terms", was fixed for fifty-five years (expiring 2022) in an area of 12,943 sq.km.[59] However, the consortium had no success finding commercially exploitable oil.[60]

The flourishing of the "black gold" resource and the abundance of the natural gas reserves attracted various international stakeholders to the region, especially in the zone of Jebel Dhanna and Ruwais at the west part of Abu Dhabi's mainland.

In 1971 the surge of concessions led the Government to found the Abu Dhabi National Oil Company (ADNOC), the main entity acting as a hub linking up all the government institutions and oil concessionary companies commissioned to execute the approved projects.[61]

From then on, oil and gas concessions have been guaranteed in various parts of the island, and oil was found in commercial quantities in multiple areas.

Hence, the years that followed saw the move towards an invasive construction programme and drilling sites, and new terminals for the crude oil and gas export appeared across the sandy dunes and along the sea shore. These are the years (1970–1980) of Italy's role as one of the major purchasers of crude oil.[62]

The early 1970s saw the involvement of two major Italian companies in the development of the Abu Dhabi's industrial landscape: the petrol-engineering group Saipem and Snamprogetti, a subsidiary of the Italian state oil company, Ente Nazionale Idrocarburi (ENI).[63]

Snamprogetti was already involved in projects in Abu Dhabi as it was working "on a gas sweetening plant for the Power House and Desalination plant at Muqta Bridge",[64] and was also one of the contenders to carry out comprehensive services to realize an oil refinery in Abu Dhabi.

Both Italian companies had been engaged in the development of important facilities for the industrial town of Ruwais, some 240 km west of Abu Dhabi itself.

Ruwais and its industrial features

In 1970 this rural desert town was chosen as site of the industrial city of Abu Dhabi Emirate and conceived as an "urban hub" for the growing population of ADNOC staff.[65]

Its original masterplan, developed by Consultant Arthur D. Little in 1978, was centred around the construction of a gas liquefaction plant handled by Abu Dhabi Gas Industries (GASCO) and other facilities such as a fertilizer plant, a new export refinery, a petrochemical complex, a marine terminal, and a sulphur handling terminal.[66] Furthermore, the producing units at the Bu Hasa, Asab, Murban (Bab), and Sahil fields would be connected directly to the Ruwais facilities.[67]

Gas processing plant

Eight years later, the gas processing plant was still under discussion, and Saipem was one of the possible leading contenders for the design, procurement, and supervision to build a gas loading jetty (one of the five parts into which the project was divided).[68]

Later in the same year, Saipem was assigned the plant, which became operational in 1981 with a production of "800 million cubic feet per day of associated gas from Abu Dhabi's onshore oil fields, for the production of liquefied petroleum gas and condensates, mainly for export".[69]

Oil refinery

The Ruwais Refinery was a central project, which involved Snamprogetti as the main consultant, and was built at the cost of 1,900 million dirhams (almost 500 million dollars), with an expected average production of 120,000 barrels per day (bdp).[70] Initially due to be completed in 1980, the refinery was finished in 1981 and officially opened in 1982, the same year in which Sheikh Zayed inaugurated the new city of Ruwais.[71] In 1985 the Ruwais refinery underwent a further expansion with another upgrade in 1997 awarded to Snamprogetti as lead contractor and for the completion of all project stages.[72]

Since 1970 Saipem and Snamprogetti have carried out numerous large-scale engineering projects onshore and offshore, making them the leading oil and gas contractors in the emirate through their subsidiaries. In 2008 Saipem acquired Snamprogetti and headed many of the most important and large-scale engineering, procurement, and construction (EPC) projects in the UAE, notably the Shah Gas Development Programme and the first UAE railway system.

Petrochemical plant

In its original masterplan, the industrial development of Ruwais furthermore included the construction of a petrochemical plant. Postponed for a few years from its initial envisaged opening date, the first major petrochemical complex – Borouge – was set up in 1998 and came on stream in 2001.[73]

This achievement in the industrial sector of Abu Dhabi required the participation of another well-known Italian company, Maire Tecnimont, which became the main contractor for the polyolefins unit plant.

Having a long successful history with the UAE – as one of the Group's sister companies realized some refining units in the area at the end of the 1970 – Maire Tecnimont has since then strengthened its presence, realizing several high-profile projects that support the UAE petrochemical value chain, which included also the consecutive expansions projects of the Borouge complex in 2007, 2010, 2018 with the recent one, Bourouge 4, awarded in 2021.[74]

The facilities of Ruwais included a sulphur handling terminal in the project, expanded with the construction of a new sulphur forming handling and export conveying system for GASCO that was assigned to Italy's Techint Engineering and Construction.[75]

Sulphur plant

The new greenfield Ruwais Sulphur Handling Terminal-2 plan was completed in 2012 and marked a new achievement for the company that had recently inaugurated its presence in the Emirates.

Heavy industries

Having as its objective to diversify its industrial economy and therefore reduce its dependence on oil and gas revenue, Abu Dhabi continued the investments not only in the petrochemical but also in the heavy industry. In this regard, the important construction project expansion of a heavy section steel rolling for the Emirates Steel Plant was envisioned and was carried on by the Italian manufactures Danieli.

Abu Dhabi and Dubai;
a different outlook

While Abu Dhabi industrial sector is more tied to hydrocarbon development and in a diversified economy based on petrochemical projects, natural gas sectors, heavy industry, the Emirate of Dubai has always had a distinct outlook. Here oil was discovered later and in smaller quantities than neighbouring Abu Dhabi in 1966. Therefore, the city had to rely on other resources to secure wealth and diversify its economy. Since 1970 Dubai used the wealth from oil exploitation to invest in infrastructure, and meanwhile strengthened and expanded its role as a key entrepôt in the region, as it had been since before the British arrival along the coast.[76]

In fact, Dubai has been a place of trade and commerce since Antiquity, its modern development has pivoted on large industrial-engineering projects that attract and facilitate trade, bringing capital.[77]

Jebel Ali Industrial Zone

In the middle of the 1970s Dubai centred its industrial production on the development of the Jebel Ali Port, a vast industrial complex 35 km southwest of the city.

Envisioned by Sheikh Rashid bin Saeed Al Maktoum, it is the major man-made artificial port of the Middle East. Its construction, contracted to the consultant Halcrow International Partnership at a cost of $1,6 billion, was completed in 1982 and comprises various industrial and residential facilities.[78]

Power and water plant

Among the major industrial facilities/infrastructure projects that the Jebel Ali area hosts is the notable Jebel Ali Power and Desalination Plant, one of the largest in the UAE.

The plant owned and operated by Dubai's Electricity and Water Authority (DEWA), went into operation in 1976. Over the years it has undergone various expansions to address the growing demand of Dubai's energy and water consumption, and most of its development is due to the contribution of important Italian companies working in the field of energy and desalination plants, such as Ansaldo Energia and Fisia Italimpianti.

Ansaldo Energia, historically present in the United Arab Emirates in the early 1990s, has always been committed to supporting the power generation service needs of the region. It was involved since the early phase of the plan developments in Jebel Ali.

While Fisia Italimpianti, an expert leader in the sustainable design and execution of water treatment, and desalination plants, started its involvement in 1999 and today it oversees eight desalination units in Jebel Ali.

Both companies were entrusted with other projects related to the power and desalination plants as Mirfa and Tawellah in Abu Dhabi, the latter became a natural gas and water desalination and power complex in a new industrial zone, between Abu Dhabi and Dubai.

Italengineering – Studio Geotecnico Nesti is another company which is worth mentioning, as it contributed to the remarkable Jebel Ali project, providing its long-standing expertise in geotechnical consulting, soil investigation, dewatering system for potable water pipelines terminal and infrastructures. Since 2007 it has been present in the UAE as a consultant for various projects related to the energy sector, also in the other Emirates of Ras Al Khaimah, Fujairah and Abu Dhabi.

Jebel Ali has also been the core of manufacturing for Dubai. The UAE industrial sector grew thanks to the establishment of the Jebel Ali industrial Free Zone in 1983, which brought in various foreign companies seeking for local contracts.[79] The Jebel Ali free zone (Jafza), is one of the largest worldwide, and today hosts over 8,000 companies.[80]

Renowned Italian companies in the energy and oil sectors played an important role in shaping the industrial landscapes of the Emirates since the formation of the country. Over the years these companies developed remarkable projects in which they are still engaged to this day, and which marked the birth of the UAE industrial cities, as Jebel Ali in Dubai and Ruwais in Abu Dhabi. They contributed to the Emirates oil and non-oil sector development and its pursuing of a strategy towards a diverse and open economy, not dependent from hydrocarbons.

With their innovative technology and sustainable approach, key elements in the UAE's governmental vision for industrialization, Italian companies continue to support the UAE's economic development philosophy, which recognizes industrialization as the main driving force towards a sustainable national economy.[81]

[1] The National Archive: www.na.ae, https://www.na.ae/en/archives/historicalperiods/emirateserasofcivilization.aspx (accessed 1 March 2022).

[2] J. Charpentier, "Cesare Di Federici and Gasparo Balbi", *Geografiska Annaler*, vol. 2 (Taylor & Francis, on behalf of Swedish Society for Anthropology and Geography, 1920), vol. 2, pp. 146–61.

[3] R. F. Nyrop et al., American University (Washington, D.C.) Foreign Area Studies, *Area Handbook for the Persian Gulf States,* DA Pam 550–185 (Washington: US Government Printing Office, 1977), 1st ed., pp. 21–22. The Republic of Venice had always conducted a lively maritime trade with the Muslim world overlooking the Red Sea, as Venice was the main power on the Mediterranean. See S. Carboni, T. Kennedy, and E. Marwell (eds.) "Venice and the Islamic World: Commercial Exchange, Diplomacy, and Religious Difference", in *Heilbrunn Timeline of Art History* (New York: The Metropolitan Museum of Art, 2000) http://www.metmuseum.org/toah/hd/cedr/hd_cedr.htm (March 2007; accessed 1 March 2022).

[4] Letters and diaries are important documents that record a country's history, geography, and culture. The travel diaries of Italian missionaries and merchants helped create a valuable body of work on Arabia and the Indies. Besides the travelogue of Gasparo Balbi (digital consultation), I was able to physically consult: V. M. Murchio, *Il viaggio all'Indie orientali del padre F. Vincenzo Maria di S. Caterina da Siena* (Venice: Appresso Giacomo Zattoni, 1678), and A. Legrenzi, *Il pellegrino nell'Asia: Cioe 'Viaggi Del Doctor Angelo Legrenzi Fisico, e Chirurgo, Cittadino Veneto: Con li Ragguagli dello Stato della Santa Città di Gierusalemme, Bethelemme, Nazareth, & altri luoghi Santi, e Città Maritime,* 2 volumes in 1 (Venice: Domenico Valvasense, 1705). Furthermore, for an in-depth reading regarding Italian travellers in the Far East, see A. De Gubernatis, *Storia dei viaggiatori italiani nelle Indie orientali, compilata da Angelo de Gubernatis. Con estratti d'alcune relazioni di viaggio a stampa ed alcuni documenti inediti,* (Livorno: F. Vigo, 1875).

[5] As reported by J. Schwartzberg in *Journal of the American Oriental Society,* Balbi was probably born in Venice about 1550. J. E. Schwartzberg, "Review of The Historical Geography and Topography of Bihar", by M. S. Pandey, *Journal of the American Oriental Society*, vol. 85, no. 3, p. 476. https://doi.org/10.2307/519518. However, the exact year of birth and death of Gasparo Balbi are unknown. See J. Charpentier, "Cesare Di Federici and Gasparo Balbi." *Geografiska Annaler*, vol. 2 (London: Taylor & Francis, on behalf of Swedish Society for Anthropology and Geography, 1920), vol. 2, p. 147.

[6] G. Balbi, *Viaggio dell'Indie orientali* (C. Borgominieri, 1590), pp. 49–50. Scanned by Claudio Ruggeri, Opal Libri Antichi, University of Turin. Internet Archive (www.archive.org).

[7] I. Abed and P. Hellyer (eds.), *United Arab Emirates: A New Perspective* (London: Trident Press, 2001), p. 74.

[8] B. J. Slot, *The Arabs of the Gulf, 1602–178: An alternative approach to the early history of the Arab Gulf states and their relations with the European powers, mainly based on sources of the Dutch East India Company* (Leidschendam, Netherlands: 1995), 2nd ed., p. 39.

[9] https://abudhabiculture.ae/en/experience/cultural-landscapes-and-oases/sir-bani-yas-island (accessed 6 February 2022).

[10] The Bani Yas was the most numerous tribal confederations in the Al Dhafra region. Then it moved from the hinterland to the Abu Dhabi coast for economic, geographical, and political factors, probably as an understanding of the potential and advantages behind being on the coast. From Qasr Al Hosn permanent exhibition. www.qasralhosn.ae.

[11] A detailed record of the tribes of the Bani Yas confederation is provided by Faruke Heard Bay in her book *From Trucial States to United Arab Emirates: A Society In Transition* (Dubai: Motivate, 2004), pp. 18–125.

[12] With the agreement of Perpetual Maritime Truce in 1853, established between Britain and the sheikhdoms, the British secured their transport and communication channel to India. Even if their intention was not controlling the commercial and affairs of the Trucial States, the formal Exclusive Agreement with the Sheikhs in 1982 automatically precluded alliances with any other foreign power. See D. Howley, *The Emirates: Witness to a Metamorphosis* (Wilby, Norwich: Michael Russell, 2007), pp. 10–15. For further details of the relationships between Britain and the Trucial States, see D. Hawley, *The Trucial States* (London: Allen & Unwin, 1970), pp. 126–85. F. Heard-Bey, *From Trucial States to United Arab Emirates: A Society In Transition* (Dubai: Motivate, 2004), pp. 279–332.

[13] R. El Mallakh, *The Economic Development of the United Arab Emirates*, RLE Economy of Middle East, vol. 13, (London: Routledge, Taylor and Francis Group, 2015), p. 20.

[14] C. Davidson, *Abu Dhabi: Oil and Beyond* (New York: Columbia University Press, 2009), p. 7.

[15] D. Hawley, *The Trucial States* (London: Allen & Unwin, 1970), p. 197.

[16] D. Heard, *From Pearls to Oil: How the Oil Industry Came to the United Arab Emirates* (Motivate Publishing, 2011), p. 37.

[17] Y. Elsheshtawy "Cities of sand and fog: Abu Dhabi's global ambitions", in *The Evolving Arab City: Tradition, Modernity and Urban Development*, edited by Y. Elsheshtawy (London & New York: Routledge, 2008), p. 259.

[18] British Political Agents were officials, representative advisers in the Trucial States. For a brief insight, see A. Reem Bani Hashim, *Planning Abu Dhabi: An Urban History* (Routledge, 2019), pp. 26–27.

[19] J. M. Al-Mehairi, *The Role of Transportation Networks in the Development and Integration of the Seven Emirates Forming the United Arab Emirates, with Special Reference to Dubai* (PhD diss., Durham University, 1993), pp. 34–75.

[20] Arabian Gulf Digital Archive (AGDA), The National Archives of the UK (TNA), Foreign Office (FO) 371/168937, *1963, Airstrip construction.* Letter, Political Residency, Bahrain, 2 October 1963, from J. R. Rich to D. J. McCarthy (Arabian Department Foreign Office), www.agda.ae (accessed 18 January 2022). AGDA, NA, FCO 371/168937. Telegram no. 848, 25 September 1963, from foreign office to Bahrain, www.agda.ae (accessed 18 January 2022).

[21] AGDA, TNA, FO 371/168937, *1963, Airstrip construction.* Letter, Political Agency Abu Dhabi, Trucial States, 23 September 1963, from J. E. H. Boustead to J. R. Rich, Political Residency Bahrain, www.agda.ae (accessed 18 January 2022).

[22] M. M. Al Serkal (4 April 2008), "Mapping the future. Italian Civil Engineer arrived decades ago", *The Gulf News.* www.gulfnews.com (accessed 18 November 2020). As reported in the article, the Italian company Zompi was then sold to Khansaheb, where Cantalupo continued his career.

[23] M. Maclean, *Spies, Subversion, and Skulduggery: The Thrilling story of the UAE's First Paved Road*, 10 May 2016, NYU-AD Institute: https://www.youtube.com/watch?v=LlIcNKvbkJk.

[24] M. MacLean, *Spatial transformations and the emergence of the national': infrastructures and the formation of the United Arab Emirates, 1950–1980* (PhD diss., New York University, 2017), pp. 213–14.

[25] Founded in Rome in 1979, Sauti Srl is an Italian company specialized in civil engineering. Since 2005 it has been part of the Bonifica Group. https://www.renardet.net/index.php/company-profile/our-international-group

[26] The United Arab Emirates, when established in 1971 were six states given that Ras Al Khaimah joined later in 1972.

[27] www.mofaic.gov.ae (accessed 15 February 2022).

[28] Ministero degli Affari Esteri, "UNIONE EMIRATI ARABI – Visita del ministro degli esteri dell'Unione Emirati Arabi a Roma", *1974 Testi e Documenti sulla Politica Estera dell'Italia*, Servizio Storico e Documentazione, Rome, pp. 331–32. www.farnesina.ipzs.it

[29] This was affirmed in a meeting of the Italian Minister Ossola in Abu Dhabi in November 1978 regarding the economic relations between the two countries, and how to extend their fruitful collaboration. Ministero degli Affari Esteri, Servizio Storico e Documentazione, "EMIRATI ARABI – Visita del ministro del Commercio estero dott. Ossola", *1978 Testi e documenti sulla politica estera dell'Italia,* Ufficio Studi, Rome, p. 181. www.farnesina.ipzs.it

[30] O. Duncan and S. Tomic, "Abu Dhabi, UAE", in *Architecture and Globalisation in the Persian Gulf Region*, edited by M. Fraser and N. Golzari (England: Ashgate, 2016), p. 129.

[31] The Emirates Center for Strategic Studies and Research, *With United Strength: HH Shaikh Zayid bin Sultan Al Nahyan, the Leader and the Nation* (Abu Dhabi: The Emirates Center for Strategic Studies and Research, 2005), pp. 243–61.

[32] Ibid, pp. 204–6.

[33] To know more about the history of this pioneering Italian company, founded in

Italy, I suggest reading the company's book *La bellezza e il tempo. Sgaravatti 1820 – 2020. Duecento anni di florovivaismo italiano* by S. Romano and R. Sgaravatti (Edizioni LSWR, 2020). There are also insights on the Arabian experiences of its leader, Leone Sgaravatti, with various recollections of this interesting project. The presence of this company is also mentioned in Ministero degli Affari Esteri, Servizio Storico e Documentazione: "EMIRATI ARABI – Visita del ministro del Commercio estero dott. Ossola", *1978 Testi e Documenti sulla Politica Estera dell'Italia,* Ufficio Studi, Rome, p. 181. www.farnesina.ipzs.it

[34] *Father of Our Nation: Collected Quotes of Sheikh Zayed Bin Sultan Al Nahyan* (Motivate Publishing, 2017).

[35] H. Salloum (27 May 1997), "How Sheikh Zayed turned the desert green", *The Christian Science Monitor*, www.csmonitor.com (accessed 5 August 2020).

[36] A. Axon, S. Hewitt (eds.), *United Arab Emirates 1975/76-2018* (Leiden: Brill, 2019), pp. 242, 474. http://www.italconsult.com/en/projects-category/united-arab-emirates (accessed 9 November 2020).

[37] The hospital opened later than expected due to the shortage of technical personnel, as reported in the Memorandum dated 13 September 1983 in the file 14 "FEAL 1982, 1985", p. 4. On https://patrimonio.archivio.senato.it/inventario/scheda/bettino-craxi/IT-AFS-020-000892/feal#lg=1&slide=2 (accessed 2 December 2021).

[38] The Emirates Centre for Strategic Studies and Research, *With United Strength: H. H. Shaikh Zayd Bin Sultan Al Nahyan, the Leader and the Nation* (Abu Dhabi: The Emirates Centre for Strategic Studies and Research, 2005), p. 250.

[39] J. Dennehy (22 Feb 2019), "Glory Days return for Abu Dhabi Hotel that once hosted Queen Elizabeth II", *The National:* https://www.thenationalnews.com/uae/heritage/glory-days-return-for-abu-dhabi-hotel-that-once-hosted-queen-elizabeth-ii-1.828561 (accessed 1 March 2022).

[40] https://www.szgmc.gov.ae/en/sheikh-zayed-and-grand-mosque (accessed 16 February 2022).

[41] https://zayedaward.org/en/about-legacy (accessed 23 February 2022).

[42] C. Davidson (19 February 2007), "The Emirates of Abu Dhabi and Dubai: Contrasting roles in the international system", *Asian Affairs* 38:1: 33–48.

[43] J. C. Henderson (18 January 2006), "Tourism in Dubai: Overcoming barriers to destination development", *International Journal of Tourism Research 8* (2): 87–99, (www.interscience.wiley.com)

[44] Y. Elsheshtawy, *Dubai: Behind an Urban Spectacle* (Routledge, 2010), pp. 102–70; 123–24; 128–29; 13–34.

[45] Abu Dhabi Urban Planning Council, *Plan Abu Dhabi 2030: Urban Structure Framework Plan* (Abu Dhabi: Urban Planning Council, 2007), p. 16.

[46] A. Haxon and S. Hewitt, *United Arab Emirates 1975/76–2018*, Contemporary Archive of the Islamic World, vol. 2 (Leiden & Boston: Brill, 2019), p. 352.

[47] O. Bouman, M. Khoubrou, and R. Koolhaas et al., *Al Manakh: Dubai Guide, Gulf Survey, Global Agenda.* (Netherlands: Stichting Archis, 2007), p. 66.

[48] R. Sharpley, "Planning for Tourism: The Case of Dubai", *Tourism and Hospitality Planning & Development* 5, no. 1 (2008): 13–30.

[49] "Dal luglio 2006 al gennaio 2008 le commesse acquisite da imprese italiane sono pari a quattro miliardi e 492 milioni di euro, mentre dal 2002 al giugno 2006 questo dato ammontava a circa 4 miliardi e 990 milioni di dollari USA". A. Lerbini, (18–23 February 2008), "Le imprese sbarcano negli Emirati", *Il Sole 24 Ore (Edilizia e Territorio,.* p. 7.

[50] www.prysmiangroup.com.

[51] R. Koolhaas, T. Reisz, M. Gergawi, B.I Mendis, and T. Decker, *Volume 23: Al Manakh Gulf Cont'd*, edited by AMO, Archis, Pink Tank, and NAi (Netherlands: Stichting Archis, 2010), pp. 42–43.

[52] S. Velegrinis and G. Katodrytis, "Drawing on sand: cities in the making", in *UAE and the Gulf: Architecture and Urbanism Now,* edited by G. Katodrytis and K. Mitchell, *Architectural Design* (London: John Wiley & Sons, 2015), p. 79.

[53] www.uaenext50.ae (accessed 1 March 2022).

[54] Sheikh Shakhbout bin Sultan Al Nahyan granted licences for oil exploration in Abu Dhabi in 1939. The first concession was signed on 11 January of the same year. Due to the outbreak of World War II, oil explorations were put on hold. The first shipment of crude oil left Das Island in 1960. From Qasr Al Hosn exhibition. www.qasralhosn.ae

[55] A. Reem Bani Hashim, *Planning Abu Dhabi: An Urban history* (Routledge, 2019), p. 25.

[56] AGIP was founded in Italy in 1926, with its main operative house in Milan; after 1953 it became ENI's subsidiary, and was then definitively acquired by ENI in 2003.

[57] AGDA, TNA, FO 371/185562, *1966 Oil: New Concessions.* Letter, British Political Agency Abu Dhabi, 21 May 1966, from A. T. Lamb to William Luce, G. B. E., K.C. M.G., British Residency Bahrain, www.agda.ae (accessed 21 Jan 2022).

[58] AGDA, NA, FCO 8/889, *1967 Abu Dhabi Oil Concessions.* "Petroleum concession agreement Abu Dhabi between His Highness Shaikh Zayed bin Sultan Al Nahyan, the ruler of Abu Dhabi, and Philips Petroleum company, American Independent Oil company and AGIP SpA", www.agda.ae (accessed 18 January 2022).

[59] AGDA, TNA, FCO 8/889, *1967 Abu Dhabi Oil Concessions* (accessed 18 January 2022). AGDA, NA, FCO 8/1964, *1972 Dec 22 – 1973 Dec 31. Oil Affairs in Persian Gulf* (accessed 21 January 2022). The part consulted is in the section "The oil Industry in Abu Dhabi. Part 1 – Information on the oil industry in Abu Dhabi and Part 2 – Information on oil companies operating in Abu Dhabi". Details on the agreement are on Part 2. The file is a collection of papers prepared by John Burnett regarding oil in the smaller Arabian states under the request of James R. Bretherton in order to have comments on the specific part related to Abu Dhabi, Dubai, and the rest of the UAE. James R. Bretherton to A. Reeve, Telegram on 26 January 1973, www.agda.ae (accessed 21 January 2022).

[60] AGDA, TNA, FCO 8/1964, *1972 Dec 22 – 1973 Dec 31. "Oil Affairs in the Persian Gulf".* The oil Industry in Abu Dhabi. Part 1 – Information on the oil industry in Abu Dhabi, www.agda.ae (accessed 21 January 2022).

[61] https://www.adnoc.ae/en/our-story/who--we-are (accessed 12 January 2022).

[62] R. El Mallakh, *The Economic Development of the United Arab Emirates*, RLE Economy of Middle East, vol. 13, (London: Routledge, 2015), p. 120.

[63] Snamprogetti S.p.A. was an engineering Italian oil and construction company founded in 1956 by ENI. In 2006 Saipem

acquired the company from ENI, and was incorporated into Saipem in 2008. Saipem (Società Anonima Italiana Perforazioni e Montaggi) is an Italian multinational oilfield services company, one of the largest in the world. Until 2016 it was a subsidiary of ENI.

[64] AGDA, TNA, FCO 8/1538, *1970 Jan 01–1970 Dec 31. Oil Production in Abu Dhabi.* N. J. A. Hooker to D. L. Hawkins, H. M. Treasury Great George Street London, SW1. Letter on 12 March 1970, "Financial Guarantee Committee Case no.827 – Humphreys & Glasgow Ltd. Oil Refinery Abu Dhabi", www.agda.ae (accessed 21 January 2022).

[65] www.ruwais.ae.

[66] AGDA, TNA, FCO 8/3149, *1978 Jan 01 – 1978 Dec 31, Oil affairs in the United Arab Emirates*. "Industrial development in the petroleum/gas sector Ruwais/Jebel Dhanna", May 1978, www.agda.ae (accessed 21 January 2022).

[67] AGDA, TNA, FCO 8/3149, *1978 Jan 01 – 1978 Dec 31,* Oil affairs in the United Arab Emirates. "Industrial development in the petroleum/gas sector Ruwais/Jebel Dhanna", May 1978, www.agda.ae (accessed 21 January 2022).

[68] Ibid. Information regarding the contention for NGL Jetty's construction in Ruwais are reported in a confidential document dated 5 March 1978. AGDA, TNA, FCO 8/3142, *1978, Jan 01 – 1978 Dec 3, UK/UAE Joint Committee*, www. agda.ae (accessed 21 January 2022).

[69] Bureau of Mines, *Minerals Yearbook Centennial Edition 1981*, vol. 3, Area reports: international. United States (Washington: US Government Printing Office, 1983), p. 1077.

[70] AGDA, TNA, FCO 8/3855, *1981 Jan 01 – 1981 Dec 31*. Major commercial projects in the Persian Gulf: Middle East contracts. To MED, FCO, 28 March 1981. "Project list: Oil, Gas and Petrochemicals". www.agda.ae (accessed 21 January 2022).

[71] AGDA, TNA, FCO 8/3855, *1981 Jan 01 – 1981 Dec 31*. To MED, FCO, 28 March 1981. "Project list: Oil, Gas and Petrochemicals". www.agda.ae (accessed 21 January 2022).
https://www.adnoc.ae/en/adnoc-refining/about-us/locations (accessed 21 January 2022).

[72] "Ruwais Refinery Expansion" *Hydrocarbons Technology*: https://www.hydrocarbons-technology.com/projects/ruwais-refinery-expansion/ (accessed 21 January 2022). The expansion commission to Snamprogetti has also been reported in the Italian national newspaper *La Repubblica*-Archivio (6 August 1997): https://ricerca.repubblica.it/repubblica/archivio/repubblica/1997/08/06/aziende-flash.html (accessed 19 January 2022).

[73] S. Carvalho (15 December 2001), "UAE's first petrochem plants starts", *The Gulf News*: https://gulfnews.com/uae/uaes-first-petrochem-plant-starts-1.432558 (accessed 5 February 2022).

[74] https://www.mairetecnimont.com/en/media/press-releases/maire-tecnimont-awarded-three-epc-contracts-worth-usd-35-billion-borouge-abu-dhabi-uae (accessed 5 February 2022).

[75] "Techint and Dodsal win Gasco sulphur deals" (29 December 2010), *MEED*: https://www.meed.com/techint-and-dodsal-win-gasco-sulphur-deals/ (accessed 5 February 2022). Wam (2 January 2011), "Gasco awards contracts worth Dh 4b", *The Gulf News*: https://gulfnews.com/business/energy/gasco-awards-contracts-worth-dh4b-1.739390 (accessed 5 February 2022).

[76] S. J. Ramos, *Dubai Amplified: The Engineering of a Port Geography* (Farnham UK & Burlington, VT: Ashgate, 2010).

[77] Ibid., pp. 74–75.

[78] A. Axon and S. Hewitt, *United Arab Emirates 1975/76–2018*, Contemporary archive of the Islamic world; vol. 2, (Leiden: Brill, 2019), p. 67.

[79] A. Axon and S. Hewitt, *United Arab Emirates 1975/76–2018*, Contemporary archive of the Islamic world; vol. 2, (Leiden: Brill, 2019), pp. 260–61.

[80] https://jafza.ae/about-us/ (accessed 7 February 2022). The so-called free zones are areas in which foreign investor can have the full ownership of their companies. Every Emirate has its specific free zones.

[81] From the UAE's Government Portal: https://u.ae/en/about-the-uae/leaving-no-one-behind/9industryinnovation-andinfrastructure and the UAE official portal for sustainable development goals https://uaesdgs.ae/en/goals/industry-innovation-and-infrastructure (accessed 6 February 2022).

Description

This timeline traces the involvement of Italian companies in the development of the United Arab Emirates, showing the bonds created over decades of close collaboration between the two countries. The scheme presented below maps the presence of Italian companies and architecture firms, and covers the geography and phases of their involvement. It starts with the unification of the United Arab Emirates implemented by Sheik Zayed bin Sultan Al Nahyan in 1971, and ends in 2021 with the Golden Jubilee and Expo 2020 Dubai. Despite its range, this timeline cannot account for the vast number of Italian companies and architecture firms of all sizes present in the country. Here the goal is to show the extraordinary intersection and collaboration between Italy and the United Arab Emirates over the decades. The X-axis indicates the years in question, the Y-axis the specific locations concerned.

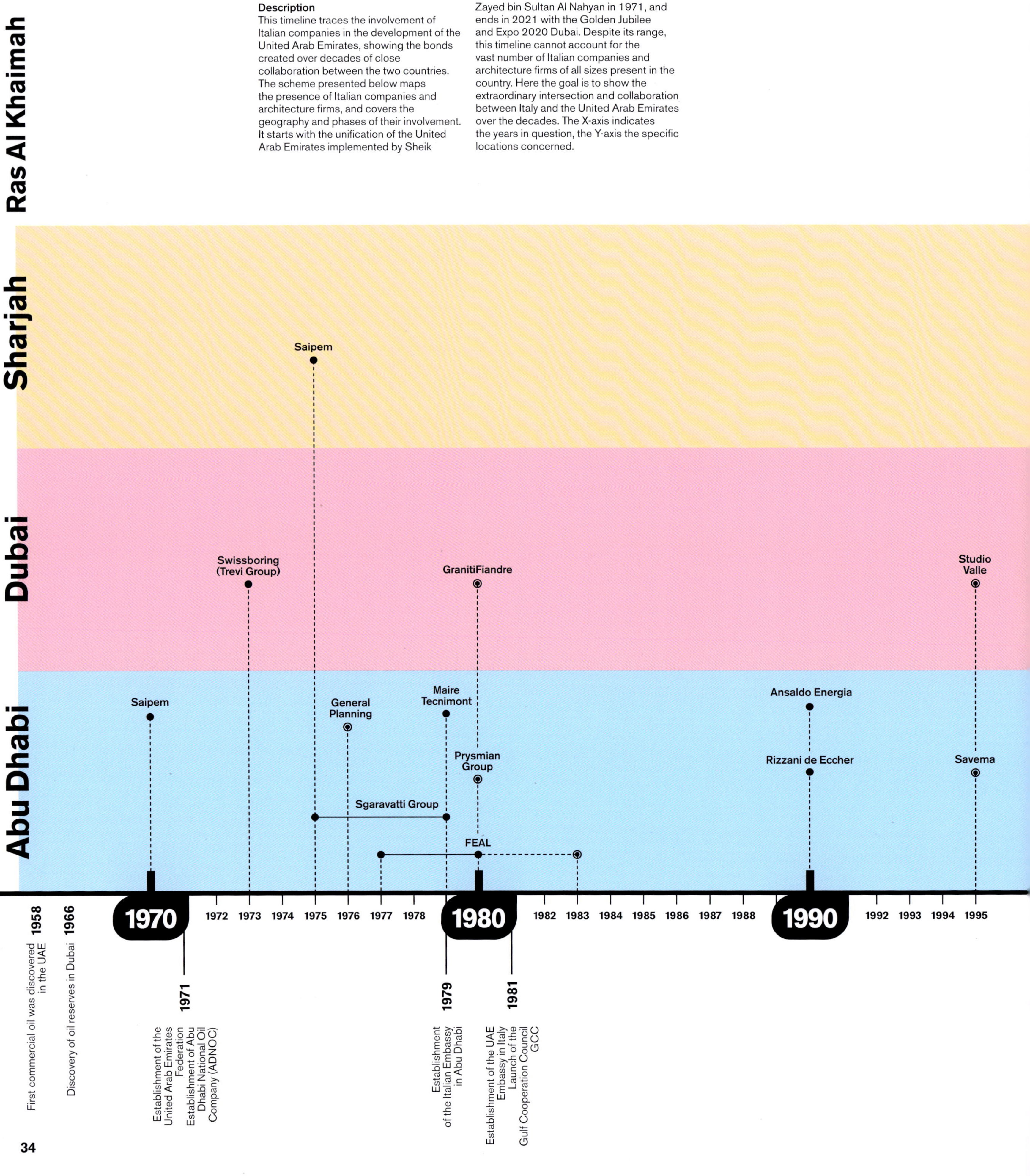

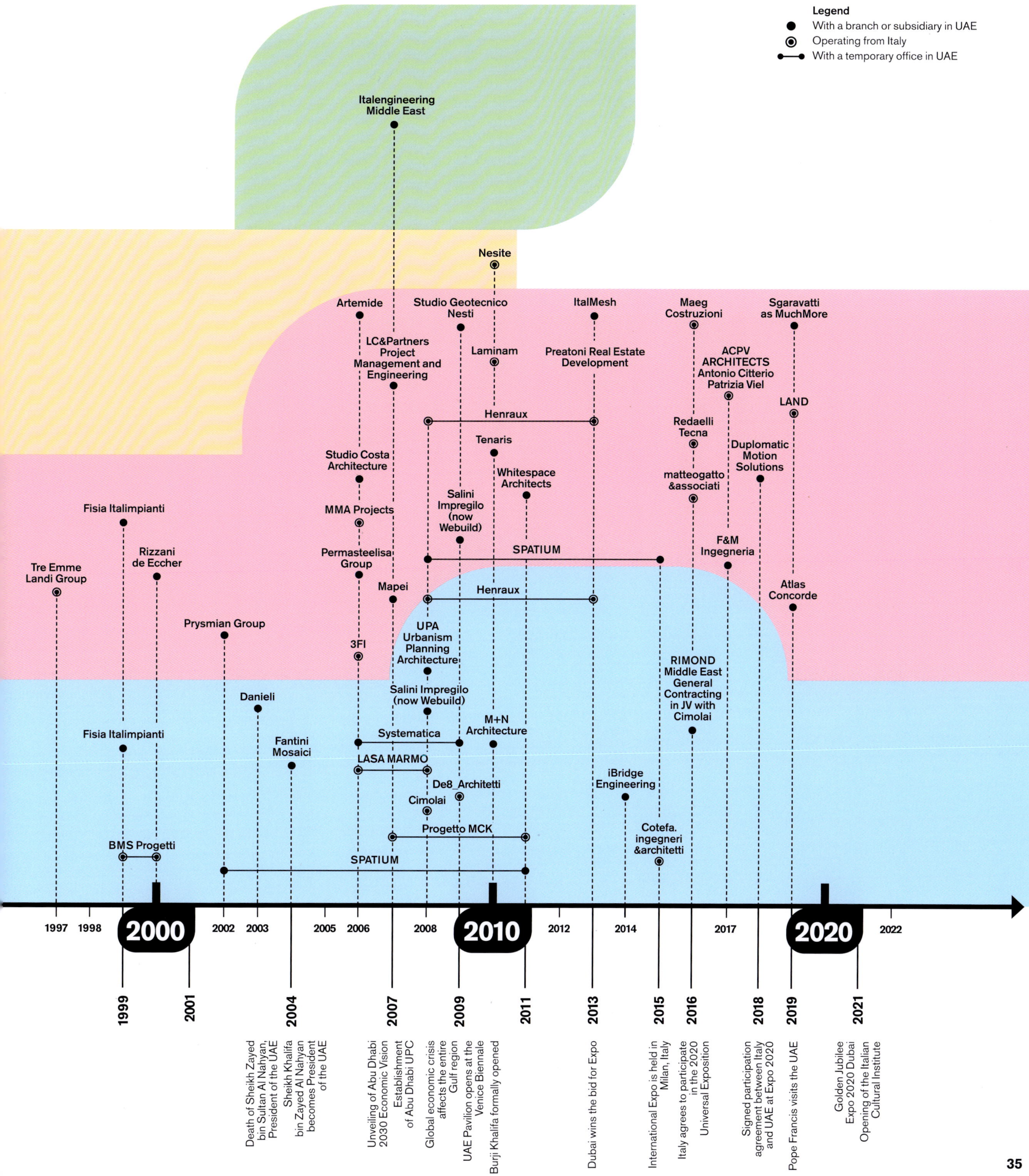
Legend
With a branch or subsidiary in UAE
Operating from Italy
With a temporary office in UAE
Italengineering Middle East
Nesite
Artemide
Studio Geotecnico Nesti
ItalMesh
Maeg Costruzioni
Sgaravatti as MuchMore
LC&Partners Project Management and Engineering
Laminam
Preatoni Real Estate Development
ACPV ARCHITECTS Antonio Citterio Patrizia Viel
LAND
Henraux
Redaelli Tecna
Tenaris
Duplomatic Motion Solutions
Studio Costa Architecture
Whitespace Architects
matteogatto &associati
Salini Impregilo (now Webuild)
Fisia Italimpianti
MMA Projects
F&M Ingegneria
Rizzani de Eccher
SPATIUM
Tre Emme Landi Group
Permasteelisa Group
Atlas Concorde
Mapei
Henraux
Prysmian Group
UPA Urbanism Planning Architecture
3FI
RIMOND Middle East General Contracting in JV with Cimolai
Danieli
Salini Impregilo (now Webuild)
M+N Architecture
Fisia Italimpianti
Fantini Mosaici
Systematica
LASA MARMO
iBridge Engineering
De8_Architetti
Cimolai
Progetto MCK
Cotefa. ingegneri &architetti
BMS Progetti
SPATIUM
1997
1998
2000
2002
2003
2005
2006
2008
2010
2012
2014
2017
2020
2022
1999
2001
2004
2007
2009
2011
2013
2015
2016
2018
2019
2021
Death of Sheikh Zayed bin Sultan Al Nahyan, President of the UAE
Sheikh Khalifa bin Zayed Al Nahyan becomes President of the UAE
Unveiling of Abu Dhabi 2030 Economic Vision
Establishment of Abu Dhabi UPC
Global economic crisis affects the entire Gulf region
UAE Pavilion opens at the Venice Biennale
Burj Khalifa formally opened
Dubai wins the bid for Expo
International Expo is held in Milan, Italy
Italy agrees to participate in the 2020 Universal Exposition
Signed participation agreement between Italy and UAE at Expo 2020
Pope Francis visits the UAE
Golden Jubilee Expo 2020 Dubai
Opening of the Italian Cultural Institute

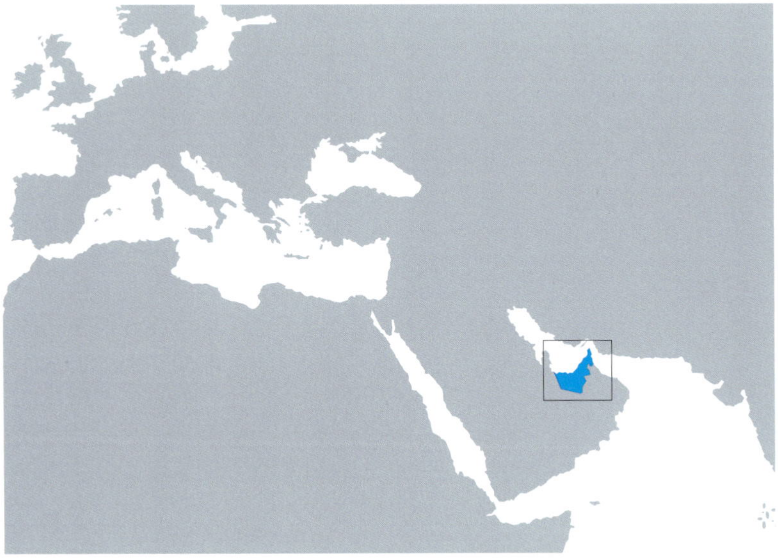

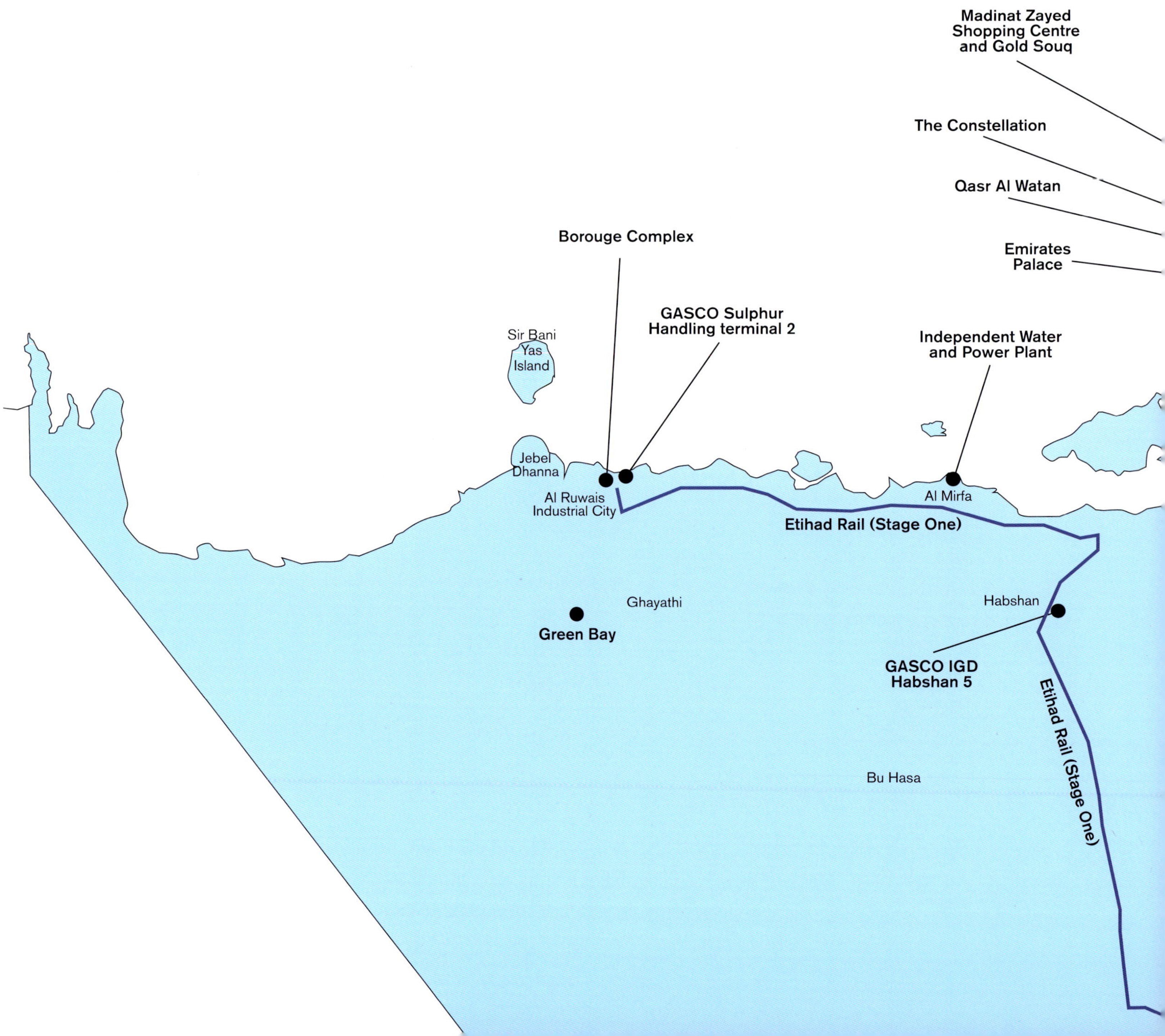
Madinat Zayed
Shopping Centre
and Gold Souq
The Constellation
Qasr Al Watan
Emirates
Palace
Borouge Complex
GASCO Sulphur
Handling terminal 2
Independent Water
and Power Plant
Sir Bani
Yas
Island
Jebel
Dhanna
Al Ruwais
Industrial City
Etihad Rail (Stage One)
Al Mirfa
Habshan
Ghayathi
Green Bay
GASCO IGD
Habshan 5
Etihad Rail (Stage One)
Bu Hasa

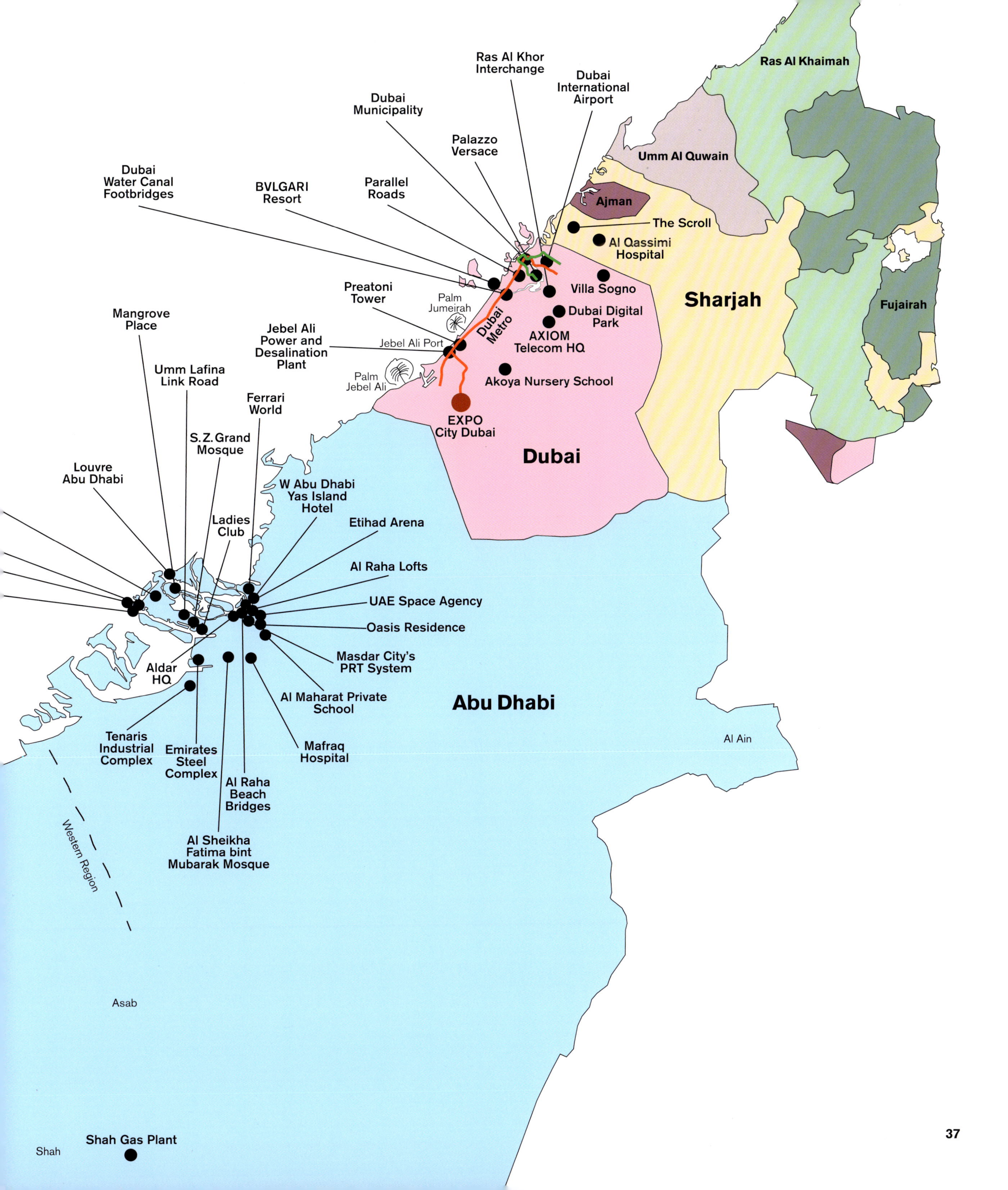

Ras Al Khaimah
Umm Al Quwain
Ajman
Sharjah
Fujairah
Dubai
Abu Dhabi
Ras Al Khor Interchange
Dubai International Airport
Dubai Municipality
Palazzo Versace
Dubai Water Canal Footbridges
BVLGARI Resort
Parallel Roads
The Scroll
Al Qassimi Hospital
Villa Sogno
Preatoni Tower
Palm Jumeirah
Dubai Digital Park
AXIOM Telecom HQ
Dubai Metro
Mangrove Place
Jebel Ali Power and Desalination Plant
Jebel Ali Port
Umm Lafina Link Road
Palm Jebel Ali
Akoya Nursery School
Ferrari World
EXPO City Dubai
S.Z. Grand Mosque
Louvre Abu Dhabi
W Abu Dhabi Yas Island Hotel
Ladies Club
Etihad Arena
Al Raha Lofts
UAE Space Agency
Oasis Residence
Masdar City's PRT System
Aldar HQ
Al Maharat Private School
Tenaris Industrial Complex
Emirates Steel Complex
Mafraq Hospital
Al Ain
Al Raha Beach Bridges
Al Sheikha Fatima bint Mubarak Mosque
Western Region
Asab
Shah Gas Plant
Shah

Urban Landscape

Green Bay

Company: Sgaravatti Group

Client: Abu Dhabi Municipality

Location: between Western Region, Abu Dhabi, UAE

Period of execution: 1975–1979

Area: 3,000 ha

Top: Leone Sgaravatti seated on the ground, talking with local people about the project.

Bottom left: Cultivation Methodology in an arid environment, 1978.
Planted in the sandy terrain, the plant is covered with a length of burlap (jute) that protects it from harsh weather. The plant is irrigated with a drip system consisting of perforated tubes placed near the plant's base, which deposit water directly to the roots, thereby avoiding evaporation.

Bottom right: Local people planting seeds in one's of the land plots assigned to Sgaravatti, 1978. Following Zayed's vision of greenery, acres of the desert have been converted into cultivated land. Tree planting and greenification have always been encouraged in the country.

Positioned halfway between Al Ain and Dubai, the so-called Green Bay continues to prosper even today, one of the oldest afforestation projects developed by the Italian leading landscaping company Sgaravatti Group.
Following the visionary idea of Sheikh Zayed to transform this part of the desert into a vast expanse of green land, Sgaravatti took part in the challenging development of a tree-planting project in the desert in the 1970s.
This commitment to greening the desert aimed to reduce the local temperature by several degrees, thanks to the evaporative cooling effect created by the greenery, creating suitable terrain for agriculture and cultivation.
Led by Leone Sgaravatti, the company spent five years in the region, which had only recently begun taking the first steps towards modernization.
The afforestation project assigned to them by the Abu Dhabi Government covered a land area of 3,000 hectares in the western region of Abu Dhabi.
Over the period 1975–76 the preliminary plantation phase was initiated, while the direct work on the sites began in 1977. At that time, new irrigation techniques borrowed from the traditional Al Aflaj[1] and furrow methods were under

experimentation in 1976 in order to enable the newly planted vegetation to resist the harsh and arid climate of the region. The new method adopted consisted of a drip irrigation system whereby a network of pipes under pressure convey water directly to the plants' roots, keeping the soil moist, while ensuring low salt levels.
Considering the lack of material to cover the designated areas, all the equipment necessary for the plantation, such as terrain, irrigation pipes, etc., was imported by the company directly from Italy.
A variety of plants were carefully selected and assessed for their ability to resist and adapt in a desert environment, these included *Prosopis spicifera* (Ghaf), *Prosopis Juliflora* (Ghuaif), *Acacia Tortilis* (Samar), *Acacia arabica* (Qarat), *Ziziphus Spina-Christi* (Sider), *Acacia raddiana* (Salam). A total of 963,000 trees and shrubs were planted in the area, compromising the land of Zaba, Gttiah, Ragheib, Belgan, Abu Freda, and Jaghelia.[2]
This phase of the project was concluded in 1979, when the early stages of seedlings rooting and their vegetative growth was confirmed.
As predicted, many of the plants introduced did not survive the harshness of the climate, but this helped identify the botanical species most suited for the arid conditions of the desert.

In 2019 Sgaravatti returned to the UAE, and opened their own office in Dubai specializing in the design of lush gardens around the Emirates.

[1] Traditional irrigation system are mostly located near oases or agricultural areas. The system uses an underground channel to conduct water over long distances from subterranean sources, such as wadis and wells, to a basin and then into the surface through channels. Well known are the *aflaj* in Al Ain – known as the Green City – as the system still today supplies water in the oasis. The *aflaj* is an ancient technology used through the UAE. To know more, visit https://aard.gov.ae/en/portal/0685D15D-14C4-4813-A20E-B83500A4E766.aspx.
[2] These areas of the Abu Dhabi desert are nowadays recognized by other names; proper identification is ongoing; the areas in question are close to Ruwais.

Sgaravatti forest plantation projects, probably in the proximity of Ghayathi, Abu Dhabi Western Region, 1978.

Mafraq Hospital

Architecture Design: General Planning

Company: FEAL

Client: Presidential court of Abu Dhabi

Consultants: Sir Alexander Gibb & Partners (Reading, UK)

Location: Mafraq, Abu Dhabi, UAE

Period of execution: 1977–1979

Area: 160,000 sq.m

Top: Aerial view of the hospital site, in a desert zone 37 km south-east of Abu Dhabi city, 1979.
The hospital plan is conceived with a main central volume (medical treatment area) from which departs: the main entrance, nuclear medicine, veterinary wing, royal and VIP suites, and ward units.

Above: Entrance gate of the Hospital.

Mafraq Hospital is designed by the Italian company General Planning in Milan and subsequently built by the Italian FEAL S.p.A.[1] appointed as main contractor in 1977, which won the tender request in an international competition.
The tender included the planning, execution, and completion of equipment of a 510 in-patient general hospital delivered on a turnkey basis, and covering an area of 500,000 square metres. The hospital is a low-rise building that comprises two main blocks: a single-story treatment block (an out-patients section, an animal house, nuclear medicine department, and other administrative and services sections) and four-storey ward units.[2] Under the English consultant Sir Alexander Gibb & Partners, British standards were satisfied considering local usage and customs.
In the late 1970s, Mafraq was a desert zone 35 km from Abu Dhabi, with only the Abu Dhabi airport and a building conurbation under construction. There was no infrastructure, electricity, or water. Therefore, the construction of the hospital was quite challenging, not only for the particular climatic and environmental conditions of a place not yet developed, but in particular it demanded considerable logistical organization.
Contracting work by FEAL started in October 1977, and required twenty-six months of strict programming at the beginning, and then a more flexible phase with daily adjustments due to a high number of unexpected events.
The executive stage consisted mainly of primary infrastructures (such as water tanks, generators, way-in roads, and internal roads, drainage, and distribution networks), housing for the Italian technicians and local workers, the prefabrication and the production of polystyrene plants, a workshop for producing ducts for the air-conditioning system.
The prefabricated components for the completion of the façades

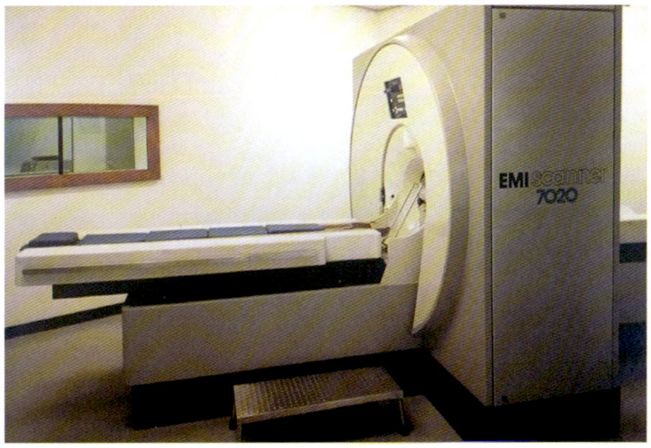

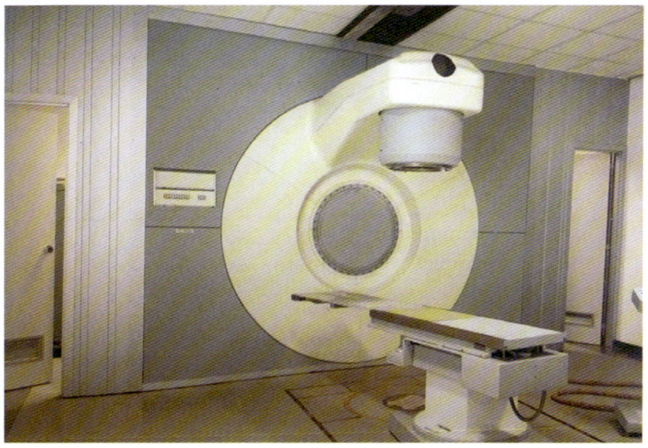

(window- and door-frames, external panels, cladding), doors, ceilings, movable partitions, and bathroom units, were supplied by the building component division of FEAL, and manufactured in factories of Milan and Pomezia (Italy).
The hospital is notable for its advanced medical equipment at the time, such as an X-ray scanner and a total body EMI-scanner for computerized tomography, the first-ever realized. The building was completed in 1979, it was not operational until 1983, when it was handed over to the Ministry of Health and officially opened.

The hospital closed permanently after twenty-five years of service in January 2020.[3] All its patients were transferred to the Sheik Shakhbout medical city (SSMC), the new clinical facility in Abu Dhabi.

[1] FEAL S.p.A. is an Italian manufacturing and construction company founded in 1945 in Milan. The Hospital Construction branch was incorporated by Impregilo (now Webuild) to then become Imprefeal.
[2] "Weekend Features. Mafraq satisfying modern medical needs" (13 July 1984), *Khaleej Times*.
[3] S. Zaman (8 January 2020), "It's the end of an era as Mafraq Hospital shuts", *The Gulf News*: https://gulfnews.com/uae/health/its-the-end-of-an-era-as-mafraq-hospital-shuts-1.68882062 (accessed 13 September 2021).

Top: Hospital ward units and royal and VIP suites, 1979.

Above: Advanced facilities for diagnosis made Mafraq hospital the country's most modern medical centre.

Left: Radiology department with a total body CT scanner.

Right: Nuclear medicine department 14 MeV Linear Accelerator.

Madinat Zayed Shopping Centre and Gold Souq

Company: Rizzani de Eccher

Client: Municipality of Abu Dhabi – Town Planning Department

Location: Abu Dhabi, UAE

Period of execution: 1992–1995

Area: 40,550 sq.m (Shopping Centre), 23,500 sq.m (Gold Souq)

Located in the heart of downtown Abu Dhabi, the Madinat Zayed Shopping Centre is a cross between a modern commercial mall and a classic *souq*.
Construction work started in January 1992 and was finished in 1995 by the Italian company Rizzani de Eccher.
The shopping centre houses a main central market and a gold *souq*, the only one in Abu Dhabi. The first is set on two floors 11.2 m high with a pedestrian area covering 38,000 square metres offering a total of 308 shops, plus a department store of 2,550 sq.m. The second is distributed over two floors, with a floorspace of 23,500 sq.m, with a total number of 231 modules for shops.
The works completed by Rizzani de Eccher also include three processing plants, elevators, spiral and linear escalators, outdoor parking lots, and assorted public meeting places, complete with electro-mechanical installations and security systems.
The two modern structures made in reinforced concrete are characterized by the fusion with vernacular elements of Islamic architecture visible externally.[1] The façades comprise a modular design of arcades and columns. These two elements form a modern reinterpretation of the *liwan*, a semi-

open passageway used as a "transitional covered outdoor space" between the interior and exterior of the building.[2]
The arcades surrounding the two buildings on its four sides facilitate the pedestrian use of the space during the day, offering shelter from the sun and heat. Decorative *mashrabiya* panels are applied along the semi-open corridor, but not in a continuum order on the arches.
Offering linkage, these passageways contribute to creating places of integration between the structures and the urban context, and act as focuses of social gathering and inclusion.[3]

The uppermost level of the buildings is equipped with traditional *barjeel* wind-towers,[4] coupled with a large dome 29-metres high covering the shopping area, and three smaller ones, 25.3 metres high (two over the gold market, and one over a shopping area), decorated with white, blue, green and azure tiles that create a geometric pattern.

[1] M. El Amrousi and F. I. AbdulHafiz, "Modern Heritage in the UAE: the Central Market/Gold bazaar – Manifestations of Neo-Islamic Architecture in the Living City", *International Journal of Advanced Science and Technology*, 29, 8s (2020): 4539–4547.
[2] M. S. S. Al-Zubaidi, *The sustainability potential of traditional architecture in the Arab world – with reference to domestic buildings in the UAE* (Doctoral dissertation, University of Huddersfield, 2007), pp.196–98.
[3] M. Pourjafar, M. Amini, E. H. Varzaneh, and M. Mahdavinejad, "Role of bazaars as a unifying factor in traditional cities of Iran: The Isfahan bazaar", *Frontiers of Architectural research*, 3, 1 (2014): 10–19.
[4] Architectural Islamic vertical element rising above the roof level, devised to funnel the air into the rooms below to provide ventilation for internal space, thereby improving the house's climatic conditions. Usually, the wind tower has a square cross-section with four vents separated by diagonal vanes, such as the one reproduced in the Madinat Zayed Mall: A. Coles and P. Jackson, *Windtower* (London: Stacey International, 2007).

Opposite: The Madinat Zayed Shopping Centre and Gold Souq in the heart of Abu Dhabi city, 1995. From the view one can note such Arab/Islamic architectural reference as the domes, the wind towers, the arches, and the eight-pointed star (octagonal) fountains.

Gold Souq façade and the courtyard at night, 1995

Dubai Municipality Building extension

Architecture Design: Studio Valle Progettazioni

Client: Municipality of Dubai

Location: Dubai, UAE

Period of execution: completed in 1995

Area: 1,600 sq.m (GFA), 16,000 sq.m (BuA)

In 1974 the Dubai Municipality awarded the development of the City Hall Complex to Pacific Consultants International, and the design was contracted to Civic Design Studio and its chief designer Kazuyuki Matsushita. Construction work started in 1976 on a total floor area of 18,625 square metres, on a site of 12,500 sq.m; construction was completed in 1979.
The design concept evolved around a large and open courtyard with a pool that unites the functions of the round council chamber, city hall, and administrative offices comprising two interlocking blocks. The first is an L-shaped building clad in white marble, and hosts the administrative offices. The second, composed from a quarter-sphere in red granite, houses the City Hall and the Council Chamber, forming a "curvilinear volume" supported on columns overlooking the central pool.[1]
The choice of the courtyard for the distribution and spatial organization reflects the use of traditional architectural elements in modern architecture to implement regionalism and express national and local identity.[2] Subsequently, this project was submitted for the annual Aga Khan Award for Islamic Architecture of 1986.[3]
In the 1990s the Italian architecture Studio Valle was contracted by the Dubai Municipality to design the extension and the linking structure of the existing building.
The project intended for office use consists of eight storeys and a basement, covering a built up area of 16,000 square metres.
Creating the extension of this remarkable architectural building was a very delicate operation, and required relating harmonically with the architecture nearby, particularly regarding the colour scheme, the volume itself, and not least the materials to apply.
The architectural language employed by Studio Valle is notable for its clarity and volumetric rigour: a modular square-mesh structure in reinforced concrete with flat slabs on a 6m by 6m plan. The solid building envelope is designed with linear elements, with set-back windows to shield the glass from the sun's rays. The top two floors, which formed the terminal building and were then modified during the construction, have vertical rectangular windows equipped with high-performance glazing.
The focal point of the entire building façade is the hollow space, an internal open court entirely covered with glazed windows where different arboreal species grow.
Internally, the vertical distribution consists of three staircases, three elevators for the public and employees, and a separate service elevator.
The offices are arranged around the perimeter of the building, with the interior windows of the office wings looking onto an internal courtyard full of trees, the core of the entire building.

[1] 1 S.S. Damlūji, *The Architecture of the United Arab Emirates* (Garnet Publishers, 2006), pp. 54–57.
[2] B. Boudiaf, "On Ecology and Culture: Analogy between Contemporary and Traditional Architectures in the Gulf Region", *International Journal of Science and Technology*, 4: 7 (2015).
[3] S.S. Damlūji, *The Architecture of the United Arab Emirates* (Garnet Publishers, 2006), pp. 54–57.

Extension of the Dubai Municipality
by Studio Valle.

Emirates Palace

Companies: Savema, Tre Emme Landi Group, Atlas Concorde

Architecture Design: Wimberly Allison Tong & Goo (WATG)

Client: HAZ Marble U.A.E. – Savema in JV with Campolonghi

Contractor: Ascon Marble & Granite

Location: Al Ras Al Akhdar, Abu Dhabi, UAE

Period of execution: 2001–2005

Today the Emirates Palace is one of the most luxurious 5-star hotels in the world, though it was originally conceived for the Gulf Cooperation Council (GCC) to accommodate state visitors and emirs on official visits.
Owned by the Abu Dhabi Government, this was essentially the first government palace that the general public was permitted to enter.
The complex was designed by the international firm Wimberly Allison Tong & Goo (WATG), which won the international design competition waged between three architectural firms. WATG's primary speciality is the design of luxury hotels and leisure, and the result is a truly majestic monumental building.
The Palace is composed of three parts. The main body – a conference centre and guest palace – plus two external wings housing the hotel, comprising a total of 394 units, including 92 suites and 22 residential suites for heads of state. Among the amenities provided are conference facilities with 40 meeting rooms; a ballroom; an auditorium; international restaurants; fitness centres, a spa, business units, and a media centre, a beachfront, and a broad range of entertainment options.[1] The entire complex spreads over 243,000 sq.m.
The architecture is massive. It is based on the geometric and harmonic proportions of the Golden Ratio, incorporated with intricate traditional decorative Islamic motifs. No fewer than 144 domes of different sizes decorated with mosaics and gold adorn the Palace; the largest one has a diameter of 45 metres and crowns the main building.
The opulent style is evident in the material used as natural stone (including marble and granite), gold-foil and mother-of-pearl. The external envelope of the Emirates Palace is entirely clad in granite stone – supplied by the Italian company Savema – in colours referencing the desert dunes of Al Ain. The company provided different granites quarried from all over the world in various shades of pink and red, with different texture finishes: Salisbury Pink, Red Royal, the pink Juparanà from India, and the red Jacaranda from Brazil. A total of 100,000.00 sq.m of granite was gathered and shipped over ten months to the main contractor.
Two other Italian companies provided the stone material for the realization of the project.
Part of the large external patio, the interior flooring, as well as the interior wall cladding of the Palace, are covered with precious marble supplied by Tre Emme Landi Group. The Dark Emperador marble with its dark brown colour with white crystals and veins, is juxtaposed with onyx (30,000 sq.m) and the creamy orange with red-streaked Crema Valencia marble (supplied 33,000 sq.m). The combination is evident in the marble-clad walls of the main building.
All the external paving for the walkaways, cycle paths, and pedestrian zone around the Palace are composed of 30,000 sq.m of porphyry from the Dolmen Collection in its traditional colours of white, pink, and grey by Atlas Concorde, Premium Italian Tiles Manufacturer. They are posed in different sizes in order to create a geometrical pattern that defines the space.

[1] From the online portfolio database of *Architizer*: https://architizer.com/projects/emirates-palace/ (accessed October 2021).

The opulent Emirates Palace, a mix of regional and local culture, 2010. The external envelope in reddish granite recalling the dunes has been supplied mainly by Savema, while the external flooring from Henraux and Tre Emme Landi Group.

The Sheikh Zayed Grand Mosque

Companies: Salini Impregilo (Webuild), Rizzani de Eccher, BMS Progetti, Fantini Mosaici, LASA MARMO LLC and Henraux (as Fantini Mosaici subcontractors), Mapei

Interior Design: SPATIUM

Architecture Design: Yusef Abdelki

Client: Abu Dhabi Public Works Department

Location: Abu Dhabi, UAE

Period of execution: 2002–2008 (interior design) 1996–2003 (construction),

Area: 22,412 sq.m

Bird's-eye view of the Grand Mosque, highlighting the 17,500 sq.m courtyard made of plain marble mosaic designed by Kevin Dean and realized by Fantini Mosaici, 2008.

Opposite: The Sheikh Zayed Grand Mosque, 2008.

The majestic Sheikh Zayed Grand Mosque rises in dazzling white at the eastern end of the island in the Persian Gulf.
With a footprint of 45,500 sq.m, the building is one of the largest mosques in the world.
Envisioned by Sheikh Zayed bin Sultan Al Nahyan in 1980, it was then built in his Middle Ages. The "Grand Mosque" is a landmark of modern Islamic architecture but also a traditional mosque, encompassing various reading levels. Its primary function is as a place of worship and assembly for the Muslims, but it is also a magnet for tourism, a memorial of its founder Sheikh Zayed, a centre for learning and discovery, as it also has a library.[1]
The design of the Sheikh Zayed Grand Mosque takes its inspiration from both Mughal and Moorish architecture, in particular referencing the Badshahi Mosque in Lahore and the Hassan II Mosque in Casablanca. It is clad in white marble and gold mosaics, equipped with four minarets 107 metres high, 82 domes with around 1,000 columns of various types, 142 pinnacles, and 70 monumental doors carved and decorated. The Taj Mahal is the source of inspiration for the entrance, while the interior minarets revive Andalusian atmospheres. Wherever you look, it is a masterpiece of religious art.
The architecture is a synthesis of knowledge, experience, and materials from various countries, one of which is Italy.
In 1996 after several competitive bidding and rebidding procedures, the construction contract was won by the Italian joint venture Salini Impregilo (now Webuild) and Rizzani de Eccher. These companies completed the structural works, foundations, and superstructure, while following a

change in the contracting strategy, which meant other consultants and contractors carried out the works. The development of the construction site project and the integral design of the different types of domes was the responsibility of BMS Progetti. On behalf of Salini Impregilo, BMS Progetti took over the management of the construction site technical office, which produced the "shop drawings", managed relations with the supervision of the works, and assisted on-site all the construction stages.
For the specific construction work of the domes, BMS Progetti integrally developed the design from the initial concept to the identification of technologies and construction details, working from its offices in Milan. The domes are a distinguishing feature of the mosque. They have the same design, but differ in size and position. Over the Sanctuary, there is a proliferation of thirty-two domes, with a central one that crowns the main prayer hall, having a diameter of 33 metres and rising 85 metres from ground-level.
The structures of the domes are "reinforced concrete with an external clad in white marble Sivec and glass-reinforced gypsum".[2]
The Grand Mosque was completed in 2003 as a reinforced concrete shell.
His Highness Sheikh Sultan bin Zayed Al Nahyan, Chairman of the Abu Dhabi Works Department, invited the Italian firm Fantini Mosaici to work on a confined part of the Grand Mosque.
However, later Fantini Mosaici went on public tender for the entire interior marble-mosaic work of the mosque, and proposed the architecture studio SPATIUM to realize the architecture of the interiors.
After an official presentation, the Italian architecture firm SPATIUM of Lorenzo Carmellini and Rocco Magnoli was appointed for the interior design of the mosque.
The working relationship between Fantini Mosaici and SPATIUM created a unique marvellous artwork that resulted from an extraordinary mastery and collaboration.
The concept proposed by SPATIUM for the interior design started from creating an iconological programme following the client's requirements.
The decorative syntax of the interiors rotates around the element of the pentagon and its derivatives: five-pointed stars, five-sided forms representing the cosmos, and the five pillars of Islam, the palm representing nature, and the palm of the hand who writes the book. Subsequently, the client desired to introduce the floral theme into the design of the decorative apparatus. Here, the pentagon was reinterpreted through five-petalled flowers, curved lines, giving shape to a complex decorative pattern developed in all rooms with various chromatic palettes, textures of materials, and finishes.
Almost 95% of the interiors are covered with marble, mainly white Lasa marble from Italy supplied by the Italian company LASA MARMO. The variety of marbles extracted from the Lasa White-Water quarry was the only one among the marble varieties selected worldwide to meet the requirements. LASA MARMO supplied 20,000 sq.m for the installation, and more than 27,000 sq.m of Lasa marble were processed into solid parts for design elements. Henraux, another Italian company, supplied marble, White Lasa, and polychrome marbles that have been used for

the claddings of the interior halls. The walls of the main prayer hall, measuring 150 metres long and 45 wide, were therefore dressed with 2,500 panels with different forms and floral motifs in marble Lasa Bianco and Lasa Bianco Ortles of various finishes: polished, sand-blasted, and bush-hammered, mosaics in marble and Murano glass in a variety of colours, from dark to light tones.

For the Qibla,[3] the proposal developed by SPATIUM consisted of a wall comprising three pages.[4] Two lateral parts 50 metres long mirror the facing wall with the floral pattern without the chromatics modulations. A wall section of 35 metres forms the central open page with the 99 names of Allah in "archaizing Kufic", pierced in marble panels of Bianco P, illuminated from the back, and inserted in the pentagon forms then articulated in organic vegetal ornaments inlay of white gold mosaics. The void and transparency provided by the wall lighten the structures, accentuating the metaphor of the prayer's passage in the directions of Mecca and the tree of life.

In the middle of the Qibla wall is the Mihrab,[5] the focal point that indicates the exact direction of Mecca, without inscriptions except for the name of Allah above it.

It revives a technique in a new way with a Muqarnas, a sort of

Entrance to the main prayer hall designed by SPATIUM. Marble intertwined flowers run on the walls and expand on the floor due to the high-quality craftsmanship of Fantini Mosaici. Among the hall's unique features are the glass doors decorated with transparent glass mosaic flowers in a variety of colours and shades.

Opposite: The main prayer hall (5,815 sq.m) with 96 columns in clusters of four that form the three octagonal chambers. The marble columns are decorated by Fantini Mosaici, with floral motifs in pietra dura. The Qibla wall with the gold Mirhab design by SPATIUM has 99 names of Allah inlaid in white gold mosaic. All the walls decorated with floral motifs derived from the pentagon are made of a complex texture of material and finishes of Lasa Bianco and Lasa Bianco Ortles and glass mosaic.

honeycomb in support for the vault of the Mihrab, and then, from there, curved undulations flow downwards. It is entirely made of handmade gold mosaic, piece by piece.

The pentagon theme of the five-pointed star pattern also adorns the wall of the open prayer halls to achieve the proportions and harmony to this transitional space leading to the main prayer hall.

As for the Qibla walls, they are decorated with different textures and white marble finishes, without chromatic modulations.

For the north and south entrance halls and the VIP areas, antechambers to the main prayer hall, the theme developed by SPATIUM was the "Garden of Paradise"[6] typical of Islamic culture. "The garden, almost always rectangular and bordered by high walls covered by vegetation, constitutes an area in which scents and colours blend and manifest the aspiration to the Mohammedan paradise that the Arabs try to recreate in the earthly life."[7]

The area sees an extraordinary floor laid and polished by Fantini's craftsmen with intertwining plant decorations climbing on the wall. The brilliant colours of the flower stand against the white marble.

A new technique was used to create the floral motif in the upper section: the flower inlay was made with semi-precious stones and hard stones inserted in a surface of marmorino[8] without joints.

The spreading tendrils of the plants begin their playful display at the springer level of the arches.

For the realization, these decorations made with various specially selected stones were bonded onto floors and columns with Mapei's high-performance two-component epoxy adhesive. Marble slabs and mosaic tiles were also glued with Mapei's solutions, including adhesives and grouts, to ensure a long-lasting performance over time.

The portals' windows are one of the building's unique features. They exalt the concept of transparency

and visibility. The door panels are decorated with flowers using sand-blasted glass and polychrome glass mosaic, highlighting the steel and aluminium structure built on the pattern generated by the pentacle. The portals' frame presents a sequence of pentagonal stars manually carved in the marble. The windows flood the chamber with soft light and catch the plant decoration's pulsating organic rhythm in a harmonic balance between mass and void. The lower part of the wall is dressed in engraved Lasa marble.

Flowers are also the leitmotif of the Shahan courtyard. The pavement design is a fantastic botanical creation of the British water-colourist Kevin Dean. Fantini Mosaici, in collaboration with the artist, developed the design and prepared the detailed working drawing. The entire area of about 18,000 sq.m is clad in plain marble mosaic with blossom flowers inlay in water-jet cut marble panels in the corners of the courtyard.

For its marvellous blossoming flowers that recur in all the areas, Fantini Mosaici called the Grand Mosque "The Mosque of Flowers".

[1] Robert Hillenbrand, *Poised Between the Past and the Future: The Sheikh Zayed Grand Mosque*, 9 September 2015, NYUAD Institute: https://www.youtube. com/watch?v=mVK-1SISk-IE&t=2001s.

[2] R. Hillenbrand, H. N. George, S. Abbasi, *The Sheikh Zayed Grand Mosque: A Visual Journey* (Abu Dhabi: published by Shawati under the patronage of the Execu- tive Affairs Council, and with the directives of the Abu Dhabi Authority for Culture & Heritage, 2010).

[3] Qibla is the direction towards the Kaaba in Mecca, to which Muslims turn at prayer. The Qibla wall is in a mosque facing the same direction. The worshippers do not pray against the wall but towards a point beyond it.

[4] Spatium's initial idea for the Qibla wall was six enormous pages of pure white marble suspended from the ground and detached from the walls and ceiling, perforated by the calligraphy of verses from the Qur'an. Air and light could thus permeate the pages, carrying the written prayers in the same direction as those being recited.

[5] The Mihrab is a semi-circular niche in the Qibla that indicates the direction that Muslims face when praying.

[6] The Islamic Garden is a symbol, a vision of paradise for the Arabs. Nature was *locus horridus* since it represented the desert, the negation, and the absence of life given by water and vegetation. The Arab Garden has as its aesthetic model the Koranic paradise. Its main point is the pleasure of the senses.

[7] V. La Paglia (4 February 2002), "*Il giardino nell'arte, Geometria e simbolo nel giardino islamico*," *Prometheus Quindicinale di informazione culturale*, Anno I, Numero 18: "Il giardino, quasi sempre rettangolare e delimitato da alti muri coperti da vegetazione, costituisce un'area nella quale si fondano profumi e colori e manifesta l'aspirazione al paradiso maomettano che gli Arabi cercano di ricreare nella vita terrena."

[8] Marmorino technique is a finishing obtained with lime and stone/marble powders used as plaster. The term marmorino derives from the use of this technique to recreate faux marble in various types of decorative structures; it can be natural white or coloured.

Dubai International Airport

Companies: Mapei, Permasteelisa Group,

Prysmian Group, Swissboring (Trevi Group)

Architecture Design: Aéroports International de Paris (ADP) and the Dar Al-Handasah (Terminal 3)

Client: Department of Civil Aviation (DCA)

General contractor: DAEP Dubai Aviation Engineering Projects

Location: Dubai, UAE

Period of execution: 1998–2008

Area: 145,000 sq.m (Terminal 1); 515,000 sq.m (Terminal 3)

Dubai airport, Terminal 3. The 84-section glazed façade by Permasteelisa Group, the so-called "teardrops", intersect the terminal's architecture, whose shape recalls an aircraft wing.

The construction of Dubai International Airport started under the ruler of Dubai, Sheikh Rashid bin Saeed Al Maktoum in 1959. Once it officially opened in 1960 with its "first airfield, it had a small terminal, an apron, three turning areas, and a runway on compacted sand".[1]
The first construction similar to a terminal dates back to 1970. At the time, it was a simple three-storey building offering assorted amenities.[2] During the 1970s and '80s it saw various improvements and enlargements to accommodate the increasing numbers of passengers and the city's development.
Following the new Dubai masterplan development launch in 1997, Terminal 2 opened in 1998, "increasing the capacity by 2 million passengers per annum".[3] Two years later, the launch of the renovated Terminal 1 with the opening on 15 April 2000 of concourse C – the first-ever concourse at the airport – under the name Sheikh Rashid Terminal, marked a new chapter in the story of Dubai Aviation. The new terminal greatly increased the flow of people, reaching "a capacity of 20 million passengers in 2001".[4]
Built on a total surface of 145,000 sq.m, the new structure comprises 27 flight gates, a vast range of duty-free outlets, 34 VIP areas, a hotel, a swimming pool, restaurants, parking spaces, and many other spaces for different functions. The entire construction was carried out in eighteen months only. Mapei's intervention in the construction of Sheikh Rashid Terminal involved delivering material for the cladding, consisting mainly of natural and agglomerate marble and ceramic tiles. It was a considerable commitment, not only considering the size of the new structure, but also for the sheer variety of surfaces used in the project. Mapei supplied with its products a total of 62,000 sq.m of adhesive and grout for the floor coverings. Its commitment also comprises Terminals 2 and 3.
To improve the airport's operations, Dubai's Department of Civil Aviation (DCA) planned the phase-2 expansion programme of Dubai Airport in June 2002. Divided into three major projects, it included expanding passenger facilities, including Terminal 3 (with concourses A and B), the expansion of cargo facilities, and the enlargement of airfield infrastructures.[5]
The construction of the site was well underway in 2004. Swissboring (Trevi Group) was one of the companies involved in this work, overseeing the foundation construction of a diaphragm wall, installing tieback anchors, and piling works.
Airport Terminal 3 became operational on 14 October 2008. Designed by Aéroports International de Paris (ADP) and the Dar Al-Handasah firm, it was the largest airport terminal built

as a "multi-level underground structure with over 1,713,000 sq.m of floor space, a capacity of 43 million passengers, and 22 aerobridges tailored to A380 aircraft".[6]
Terminal 3 with concourse B offering direct linkage is approximately 1 kilometre long, and its shape is similar to an aeroplane wing. The structure of 84 individual façades and two sloped cable walls at either end of the building are comprised of point-fixed glazing throughout.
The glazed façade terminates at the base with a lattice girder that acts as a structural spring.
Permasteelisa Group was involved in the realization of the façade system of the entire terminal, which entailed 35,000 sq.m of glazed tension connective systems.
Prysmian Group supplied several hundred kilometres of special fire-resistant cables for the new Emirates Airline terminal to ensure the highest levels of safety in the event of fire, and to help protect the state-of-the-art building materials.
Mapei contributed to the supply of products for the installation of the stone flooring in the concourses of Terminal 3 as well as other areas, such as the airport lounges, etc.
The public areas were fitted with around 18,600 seats and 6,800 tables designed and supplied by Centro Studi – Matteo Grassi.[7] The company had previously supplied all of the Dubai Airport's Terminals over the years, starting in 1999 with Terminal 1.[8]
Over the years further expansions and improvements were completed in order to accommodate the steady increase of passenger throughput.
Today the Dubai International Airport comprises three major terminals and four concourses. With its current capacity, DXB can oversee 92 million passengers annually. As reported in *The National*, in 2019 the airport handled 86.4 million passengers, retaining its position as the world's busiest hub for international passengers for the 6th consecutive year.[9]

1 https://www.airports-worldwide.com/united_arab_emirates/dubai_intl_united_arab_emirates.php (accessed 25 October 2021).
2 https://daep.gov.ae/en/our-airports/dubai-international-dxb/terminal-1/ (accessed 24 October 2021).
3 https://www.dubaiairports.ae/corporate/about-us/history/ (accessed 25 October 2021).
4 https://daep.gov.ae/our-airports/dubai-international-dxb/concourse-c/ (accessed 24 October 2021).
5 "Dubai International Airport (DXB/OMDB)" (27 March 2003). *Airport–technology.com* https://www.airport-technology.com/projects/dubai/ (accessed 24 October 2021).
6 https://daep.gov.ae/en/our-airports/dubai-international-dxb/terminal-3/ (accessed 24 October 2021).
7 "Dubai International Airport" (22 March 2009), *Domus*. https://www.domusweb.it/en/design/2009/03/22/dubai-international-airport.html (accessed 25 October 2021).
8 https://www.matteograssi.com/en/projects/dubai-airport (accessed 25 October 2021).
9 D. Kamel (5 February 2020), "Dubai International retains number one rank as world's busiest hub for international passengers". *The National*. https://www.thenationalnews.com/business/aviation/dubai-international-retains-number-one-rank-as-world-s-busiest-hub-for-international-passengers-1.974319 (accessed 25 October 2021).

Dubai Metro

Companies: Rizzani de Eccher, Swissboring (Trevi Group), Prysmian Group, Mapei

Architecture Design: Aedas with Atkins

Client: Roads and Transport Authority (RTA)

Contractor: Emirates Sunland Group under a joint venture with Arabtec

Location: Dubai, UAE

Period of execution: 2005–2011

Length: 74 km

The Dubai Metro is the first mass transit system fully automated in the Arabian Peninsula.
It comprises two lines, the Green and the Red, for a total length of 74 kilometres, with 47 stations. Other lines are envisaged for the future, but are not built yet.
Visible from the Sheikh Zayed Road since it runs in parallel, the stations are distinctive for their curved roof in the shape of a clamshell, referencing the region's era of pearl-fishing and gilded façades.[1]
The metro's construction and launch were very high profile, since it is a true feat of engineering and explicitly designed to serve Dubai's ever-growing and ever-changing transportation needs.
Started in 2005 and administered under the Dubai Roads and Transport Authority (RTA), the Italian firm Rizzani de Eccher was involved in various technological, engineering, and construction aspects of the lines, which cover a deck area of 593,000 sq.m.
The first section, the Red Line, runs on an elevated viaduct except for one stretch where the line runs underground (4 station). The line covers more than 52 km for a total of 29 stations (including the 2 stations connecting with the Green Line, and 1 with Route 2020), completed in 2009.

View of the elevated section of Dubai Metro. When inaugurated, it was the first urban elevated rail network in the country, and the first to run in the Gulf region, 2010.

Opposite: Dubai Metro station. The state-of-the-art designs also required the latest in construction techniques and materials, which were utilized for the first time in the region by Rizzani de Eccher and Mapei due to the project's uniqueness.

September 2011 saw the inauguration of the Green Line, which instead runs perpendicular to “U” passes in the congested central areas of the city, so it runs partly underground and partly on an elevated viaduct intersecting two different points with the Red Line. The Green Line includes 18 further stations (8 of them underground and 2 depots), which cover approximately 23 kilometres. The construction of the project also saw the participation of other expert Italian firms such as Prysmian Group and Mapei.

The Prysmian Group furnished the underground power and communication system cables to cover all functions, including fire-resistant cables to ensure continuous operation of the safety and critical circuits in the event of fire.
Mapei was involved from the very start of the project. Its UTT division (Underground Technology) engineers provided advice on many different technical aspects. As a result, Mapei supplied a specific coating to the precast tunnel segments to assure their long-term durability.

For the overground sections, Mapei played a significant role in fast-tracking the finishes to the platforms, without compromising performance.
Samples of the selected resin agglomerate (artificial stone) tiles were sent to Mapei’s R&D centre in Milan, where extensive testing was carried out to determine sensitivity to moisture and stability.
The screed was designed as a fully bonded system by the JTJV (the construction JV); thinner areas, particularly over services, were reinforced with a light steel mesh to enhance the flexing and tensile properties of the screed in those sections. Mapei’s local subsidiary provided significant support to the constructors and many of their key subcontractors. Numerous cases required substantial on-site technical assistance, such as inspections, instruction in material mixing and usage, troubleshooting, moisture content reading, etc.

[1] H. Bohle and J. Dimog (2016), *Architectural Guide: United Arab Emirates,* Berlin, Dom Publishers, pp. 268–70.

Ras Al Khor Interchange - Dubai

Company: Salini Impregilo (now Webuild)

Client: Roads and Transport Authority (RTA)

Location: Dubai, UAE

Period of execution: 2006–2009

Length: 62,000 sq.m

In 2006 Webuild was appointed as main contractor to construct the new Ras Al Khor Interchange 1, a motorway junction with three underpasses and twenty bridges directly connecting the residential area of Al Safa Road with Financial Centre Road. This project relieved traffic congestion in the central area and eased circulation, becoming a vital artery to the financial heart of Dubai. The new interchange is capable of guaranteeing a flow of up to 16,000 vehicles per hour. The area has also a significant tourist appeal, given that it hosts several of the most spectacular skyscrapers in the world, along with luxury shopping malls that are an international attraction.

Aerial view of the Ras Al Khor Interchange, devised to ease traffic flow, 2010.

W Abu Dhabi – Yas Island hotel

Interior Design: De8_Architetti + Asymptote

Architecture Design: Asymptote Architecture

Company: Permasteelisa Group

Client: Aldar Properties PJSC

Contractor: Al Futtaim Carillion

Location: Yas Marina Island, Abu Dhabi, UAE

Period of execution: 2007–2009

Area: 85,000 sq.m

W Abu Dhabi – Yas Island, hotel 2010. The iconic architecture designed by Asymptote straddles the Formula 1 Yas Marina Circuit (the second one built in the Middle East), and on the other side facing the Marina.

Opposite top: Close-up of the glazed façade built by Permasteelisa Group, reflecting the Yas Marina.

Opposite bottom right and left: Hotel interior design by De8_Architetti + Asymptote Architecture. Intangible lines and choice of materials determine the space.

The W Abu Dhabi – Yas Island is the first ever hotel and complex built over a Formula 1 racetrack. Designed by Asymptote Architecture, it comprises two glazed twelve-story elliptical buildings linked by a sculptural steel and glass monocoque bridge. An undulating grid shell like a fluttering veil encloses both buildings. This faceted surface is made of 5,800 diamond-shaped glass panels which serve to interrupt the direct sunlight. The exterior façade of the buildings is a continuous glazed curtain wall realized by Permasteelisa Group. The envelope reflects the surrounding landscape and has specific acoustic insulation to muffle the roar of the racing cars. At night, the hotel starts shimmering; the grid is transformed into a full-spectrum light show thanks to LED luminaires mounted on the lattice designed by Asymptote in collaboration with Arup lighting. The colours shift and shimmer seamlessly without compromising transparency from within the building.

The hotel interior design is a result of a successful collaboration between De8_Architetti and Asymptote. Contrary to what happens when the interior does not reflect the architecture, the project was born from a clear objective to make the inside aesthetically consistent with the outside, notwithstanding the functional logic behind every line. The interior vis-à-vis the exterior is not just a communication of literal forms, but at the same time, coherent strategies and well-orchestrated emotions to the users. The spectacular Formula 1 site does not translate parallel to how the W Abu Dhabi is spectacular on its own. On the contrary, the project's logic identifies intensely with the functional programme.

The site's internal dynamics, its ebb and flow and connective pathways, the abstract lines of the slte, are all seamlessly resolved and define the organization of the spaces and the attentive choice of materials. The materials selected for the interiors were exactingly assessed as work progressed, and although more or less traditional in nature, the resulting textures show variety and sophistication. Environmentally responsive, the materials employed are compatible with the region's most abundant resource – sunshine – and were carefully selected to provide the optimum usage of natural light, and generate an entirely new kind of interior landscape. The parametric processes determined the interior design not as mere decoration, but as an ensemble of timeless ornaments that mediates between "local" and "global", "traditional" and "contemporary".

In 2011 De8_Architetti won the interior design prize at the fourth Ischia International Architecture Prize (PIDA) for the W Hotel.

Aldar Headquarters

Companies: Swissboring (Trevi Group), Permasteelisa Group, Metra

Architecture Design: MZ Architects

Client: Aldar Properties PJSC

Main Contractor: Aldar Laing O'Rourke Construction

Location: Al Raha Beach, Abu Dhabi, UAE

Period of execution: 2007–2009

Area: 123,000 sq.m (basement included)

Aldar HQ Building, 2010.
First circular building in the Middle East and the first architecture to be completed along the waterfront development of Al Raha Beach.

Opposite: Close-up of the building's convex façades, 2017.
The junction is made with an indented glass built by Permasteelisa Group and aluminium profiles supplied by Metra. The triangular glazed pattern of the façade mirrors the surroundings.

Aldar Headquarters, the first office building completed in Al Raha Beach development, dominates the skyline with its unique shape. It is a disk-shaped, fully glazed, freestanding building, with two curved façades held together vertically, like a standing clamshell slightly ajar. The circular skyscraper designed by MZ Architects recalls the region's maritime heritage, and at the same time, "its timeless geometry is a symbol of perfection and infinity."[1]

Apparently simple in its geometric form, the building brought new challenges of stability and structure, which were overcome with the fusion between architecture and structure.

The solid ground where the building stands today did not exist before, as it was underwater. Therefore, a large operation was needed to create a stable base where the circular building now rises. The area was consolidated thanks to the creation of the building's foundation system, which was carried out by Swissboring (Trevi Group). More than 20 million cubic metres of sand were required, and pumped through the floating pipes to the construction site to create the base, consisting of marine sand. Concrete diaphragm walls 16 metres deep were built into the ground, and sand between these walls was then removed. Subsequently, 385 concrete piles were driven into the ground: half of these piles worked on friction with the soil to secure the structure to the sand. Further half-piles were driven deep into the terrain to transfer the entire load of the building to the ground. Water was pumped out continuously from the sand into the sea, to prevent waterlogging. A raft slab was cast on top of the piles in order to

reinforce the foundations, and to distribute the weight of the building in equal measure. More than 12,000 cubic metres of concrete were used to construct the raft foundations carrying the structural glass band that holds the two main sections together. From the cement podium, two separate columns of reinforced concrete act as the spine throughout the building's elevation, having a diameter of 110 metres.
The external glass shell of the building is quite singular. A revolutionary diagrid steel structure was created in order to support the façade system and achieve the building's circular shape. This system was adopted in construction in the UAE for the first time, and eliminated the need for internal columns to support the structure.
The façade's geometric skin is composed of triangular glass modules set into aluminium frameworks, whose size varies on each floor. Using this geometric shape has the advantage of sloping the sides to achieve the desired curvature. The aluminium composite cladding in front of the façade of the diagrid members is also part of the main façade's unitized system, and creates a distinctive diamond-shaped pattern.
The building envelope was designed, engineered and manufactured by Permasteelisa Group, while Metra extruded all the aluminium façade profiles by realizing 40 different types of dies.
In total, the building envelope work of Permasteelisa Group consisted of a 20,000 sq.m unitized glass façade (the main elevations oriented east–west) and 4,000 sq.m of aluminium composite sheet cladding before the diagrid members. Instead, the north–south elevation has a 1,500 sq.m unitized glass façade that yields a glazed skylight at the top of the building plus 4,400 sq.m of aluminium composite sheet cladding at the perimeter.[2] Each of the three parts has different characteristics of water-proofing and other values of inertia and capacity to absorb the oscillations of the building. Due to its challenging design, the façade's geometry was designed with parametric tools newly introduced when the project started. It was generated from a toroid cut from a cylinder to create the perfect circle in elevation.
For manufacturing the glass pieces that form the façade, Permasteelisa Group set up a movable factory near the construction site. It was the first time for the Group in its long history of major projects.
All the materials used in the building – concrete, steel, and glass – were 100% produced from recyclable materials. "The project was developed in line with the standards of the US Green Building Council LEED[3] (Leadership in Energy and Environmental Design), and it was completed in only 30 months.
In 2008 the Aldar Headquarters was nominated "Best Futuristic Design" at the Building Exchange Conference in Valencia, Spain. In 2009 was the winner of the Best Architecture Award at the CNBC Arabian Property Awards.

[1] MZ Architects https://www.mz-architects.com/projects-detail.php?prid=64&cat=Offices (accessed 24 October 2021).
[2] https://www.permasteelisagroup.com/project-detail?project=2254 (accessed 24 October 2021).
[3] "Al Dar Headquarters / MZ Architects" (4 June 2012), *ArchDaily*: https://www.archdaily.com/240524/al-dar-headquarters-mz-architects ISSN 0719-8884 (accessed 28 October 2021).

Ferrari World

Companies: Mapei, Prysmian Group, Swissboring (Trevi Group)
Architecture Design: Benoy
Client: Aldar Properties PJSC
Contractor: Aldar Properties in JV with Besix
Location: Yas Island, Abu Dhabi, UAE
Period of execution: 2008–2010 (construction); 2009–2010 (intervention)
Area: 176,000 sq.m

In the heart of Yas island, November 2010 saw the inauguration of Ferrari World, the first-ever theme park of the well-known Italian brand.
The park comprises a Formula 1 racing circuit, and a Ferrari experience for a total area of 176,000 sq.m of which 80,000 ca. are indoor.[1] It offers rich multi-sensory adventure for all visitors, embracing the legendary automotive brand's culture, spirit, and history.
A visually distinct form houses the leisure attraction designed by the British Architecture firm Benoy. With its sinuous double curve side profile, the building reflects in its shape a Ferrari GT chassis with its fiery red colour and prancing horse across the huge undulating roof structure.
The work for its construction started in 2007 and lasted three years.
The Italian Trevi Group, through its subsidiary Swissboring won the contract for the foundations.
The works comprises a diaphragm 2.2 km long for the circuit and 17,826 Nos. – 270,000 LM foundation piles for the theme park, with the value of US$ 80 million, and with production reaching up to 100 piles per day. This commission confirms Italy's recognized technological input to the project and the level of excellence achieved by Swissboring. Another important feature to the project's was the award to Prysmian Group for the supply and installation of technologically advanced cables.
Mapei products have played an essential role in constructing one of the biggest indoor theme parks in the world. With Mapei's solutions, more than 25,000 sq.m of surfaces were waterproofed in the fountains, tanks, water features, planters, and other surfaces that required sealing. An entire system of waterproofing products, accessories, and paints was applied to ensure precision performance in all the various areas of the park. PVC tiles were used for flooring the entrance and games areas, where Mapei ensured that the substrate was perfectly flat with self-levelling solutions. Porcelain, marble, and glass mosaic in the corridors, toilets, and water features were also installed with Mapei's adhesives and grouts. The prestigious project once again shows Mapei's ability in the construction sector, supplying solutions at the highest level and guaranteeing maximum quality for the work carried out.

[1] "Ferrari World Abu Dhabi / Benoy" (26 October 2018). *ArchDaily*. https://www.archdaily.com/904628/ferrari-world-abu-dhabi-benoy ISSN 0719-8884 (accessed 12 January 2022).

Abu Dhabi Ferrari World, 2017. One of the entertainment attractions of Yas Island. With the lean sinuous lines of its red roof reminiscent of a Ferrari, and a roller coaster, the theme park can be seen beyond the Yas Links Golf Course.

Masdar City's Personal Rapid Transit System

Company: Systematica

Client: Foster + Partners

Location: Masda Cityr, Abu Dhabi, UAE

Period of execution: 2008–2010

Area: 6 sq.km

Masdar City masterplan, conceived by the British architecture firm Foster + Partners, is a science and eco-city/green city designed in 2006.[1] The city's project, devised to rely solely on renewable energy sources, included the valuable input of Systematica for all the transport and mobility-related aspects. One of the key objectives was to provide residents, employees, and city users with the highest quality of life and the lowest environmental footprint in 6 km^2 of plot area, entirely reliant on renewable energy.
The driving principle behind Masdar City's concept was to ensure a fully integrated planning and design approach in which all primary elements – building design, energy generation, waste management, and transportation – would contribute to effectively achieving carbon neutrality.
To this end, the urban design plan echoes the traditional Arab city, while combining "high-tech devices for green energy performance".[2]
Accessibility throughout the complex was devised for pedestrian movement only, and is served by an extensive network of self-driving electric vehicles – Personal Rapid Transit (PRT) – originally located underneath the podium upon which the entire complex is built.
The provision of a permeable and fully integrated PRT network forms the central strategic element for the system's overall sustainable mobility strategy. Systematica contributed to the design of the entire PRT system, providing the overall operational level assessment.

Opposite: Underground PRT system conceived by Systematica to fulfil the carbon neutrality principle of the citadel.

Below: Masdar City plaza, 2012.
A traditional ancient Arab medina set out the development model of Masdar City: orientation to maximize natural ventilation, pedestrian walkways and shaded spaces that link up the plazas, courtyards, and open spaces with high permeability standards, and connectivity.

Considering the critical goal of carbon neutrality and general sustainability, the PRT represented the most suitable solution for the complex's internal transport network.
The feasibility assessment was based on the most advanced strategies and technologies for zero-impact mobility, promoting innovative solutions to be implemented for the first time in Masdar.
The system was designed to provide rail-level safety with an efficient taxi-like service by minimizing intermediate stops, thus reducing the vehicle's energy consumption; moreover, the PRT system ensured comfortable, efficient, seamless, and door-to-door trips.

Given its driverless feature, the energy-efficient and carbon-free PRT system guarantees a reduction of operational costs. At the time of writing, out of the seven planned phases of the original master plan, only the first one has been completed, the second is about to start. The first line of the PRT network was inaugurated in 2010. However, it is running as a pilot scheme and in expectation of being complemented by additional services operated by electric vehicles for freight and delivery movements. The transportation system is integrated with a dense network of pedestrian walkways, public parks, and open spaces incorporated into the city's design.

[1] The entire project of Masdar city was scheduled to be completed by 2016. However, when construction work began in 2008, the project was hit by the global economic crisis, and the schedule met with dire setbacks. For this reason, the entire project was scaled back, and many of the city's elements had to be rethought. The expected completion is now delayed to 2030, as reported in *Arabian Business*. A.Imanova (19 July 2016), "Masdar City Targets completion by 2030", *Arabian Business*: https://www.arabianbusiness.com/masdar-city-targets-completion-by-2030-639109.html (accessed October 2021).
[2] A. Andraos, "Problematizing a Regional Context: Representation in Arab and Gulf Cities", in *The New Arab Urban: Gulf Cities of Wealth, Ambition, and Distress*, edited by H.Molotch and D. Ponzini (NYU Press, 2019), pp. 58–78.

Al Sheikha Fatima bint Mubarak Mosque

Architecture Design: SPATIUM

Client: Sheikha Fatima bint Mubarak

Location: Muhammed bin Zayed City, Abu Dhabi, UAE

Period of execution: 2008–2011

Area: 16,090 sq.m

Designed by the Italian architecture firm SPATIUM, the Sheikha Fatima bint Mubarak Mosque has a unique architectural design. The building is inspired and shaped by the interaction of two geometrical forms: the spiral and the square. These forms reference the minaret of the Grand Mosque of Samarra[1] (Iraq, 9th century CE), which stands on a square base with its spiral structure.[2]

Its solid and evocative shape and great symbolic value recall the ascent to higher levels of self-knowledge and closeness to the divine.

The square shape of the prayer hall, completely free from any obstruction, maximizes the use of the space, allowing the worshippers to pray in uninterrupted lines equal in length. The area is lit from above via a spiral dome. The spiral roof, covering the entire space of the prayer hall (*haram*), provides a sense of dynamism, conveying a sense of skyward lift, a symbolic reference to the act of praying.

The dome comprises 19 panels, each separated by the next by a glazed space to provide natural lighting during the daytime and enhance the effect of upward movement. The internal open volume is completed by a square spiral-shaped chandelier that defines the space by creating a relationship between the spiral roof and the square plan of the *haram*.

The perimeter wall rises in line with the roof. The walls are at 6 metres high, behind which lie the additional functions of the building. The main one is the women's prayer room, strategically located opposite the Qibla wall and above the entrance, separate from the main *haram* by perforated panels (mashrabiyas). This allows the ladies their privacy, while simultaneously being part of the same function with the other worshippers.

Mashrabiya and calligraphy are traditional decorative elements used in many Islamic sacred buildings. The main internal wall, known as the Qibla, carries an apparently random distribution on a black background the ninety-nine names of Allah in gold. This gives the impression that the names are "floating" in the air, as if the Qibla "absorbed" the prayers and conveyed them towards Mecca.

The floor in marble mosaic comprises a gradation of colours, radiating in a swirl from the centre to the outside, where pebble stones continue the same pattern.

Seen from outside, the entire building's mass seems to float above the ground, being supported by a colonnade closed by a glazed partition enhancing the dynamism and the sense of "lift" conveyed by the spiral shape. This concept is achieved through an absolute symbiosis of structure and architecture. The structure is an integral element of architecture; besides its primary load-bearing role, the colonnade enclosure contributes architecturally to another layer of aesthetic and functional richness to design. It not only increases the enjoyment of the building, but also improves its functionality, while raising the spirits of the occupants.

The minaret adjacent to the mosque is embedded into the ground. Twisting upwards for 60 metres, the tower is clad with terracotta bricks, as are the façades, ensuring a close dialogue with the architecture of the main building. The use of terracotta cladding helps to absorb sunlight, and cools the interior by several degrees.

The shape and structure of the entire mosque and the use of rough materials make the house of worship an excellent combination of heritage and modernity, all in one.

The spiralling roof creates dynamism in the architecture's interior elevation. Black mashrabiya panels and calligraphy decorates the interior walls.

Opposite: Detail of the spiralling roof.

[1] The mosque was commissioned in 848 and completed in 851 by the Abbasid caliph Al-Mutawakkil who reigned from 847 until 861 in Samarra. It was built as a substitute for the previous mosque, which was considered too small for the worshippers and the troops. At that time, it was the world's largest mosque.
T.M. Al-Amid, "Abbasid architecture of Samarra in the reign of both Al-Mu'tasim and Al-Mutawakkil". *Annexe Thesis Digitisation Project 2016 Block4* (University of Edinburgh Press, 1978), pp. 128–31.

[2] J. Dennehy (28 May 2019), "Unique mosque brings modernism and echoes of Iraq to the Abu Dhabi neighbourhood", *The National*: https://www.thenationalnews.com/uae/heritage/unique-mosque-brings-modernism-and-echoes-of-iraq-to-abu-dhabi-neighbourhood-1.866913 (accessed 1 June 2021).

Left: Sheikha Fatima Mosque by SPATIUM, 2012. The spiral is the leitmotif of the architecture.

Right: External view, underlining the roof of dark glazing and the portico, 2012.

Al Raha Beach Bridges

Company: Cimolai

Client: Aldar Properties PJSC

Main Contractor: Aldar Properties PJSC in JV with Laing O'Rourke

Location: Al Raha Beach, Abu Dhabi, UAE

Period of Execution: 2009–2012

From 2009 to 2012, the Italian construction company Cimolai was involved in the development of the Al Raha Beach infrastructures designed to ease accessibility to the various areas over the Grand Canal. Cimolai's programme for this project included the engineering, supply, and on-site installation of six tree-lined avenue bridges and twelve boulevard bridges. These bridges offer a spectacular view of the sea and the waterfront promenade, and lead around the new residential areas.

Cimolai developed the structural design of the bridges with the support of Incide, an Italian multidisciplinary engineering firm. The avenue bridges comprise six steel arch structures of 80 metres in length, with three spans of around 20m and a width of 29.4m in order to accommodate four lanes of traffic, two docks, two sidewalks, and the central compartment for the mechanical, electrical, and plumbing ducts.
The supporting structure of each deck consists of two pairs of

Al Raha Beach is one of Abu Dhabi's largest urban developments on a reclaimed coastline, owned by Aldar Properties, the leading Abu Dhabi real estate developer, management, and investment company.

Opposite top: Avenue Bridge, construction site, 2010.

Opposite bottom: Boulevard Bridge, 2013. Cimolai engineered detail fabricated and constructed 6 Avenue and 12 boulevard bridges.

lowered circular steel arches that support a set of opened spandrels, which in turn support the upper stringer. The reinforced concrete slabs rest on the upper stringer of the arches and transoms of decreasing height. The steel structure was supplied by Cimolai, while the concrete contractor provided the slabs.
Architecturally the bridges are exposed to view, which required a level of finishing higher than that of standard structural steel.
The main structure of the boulevard bridges comprises a set of arches supporting the composite steel and concrete deck on which the roadway is laid, an external walkway, and an internal compartment for the mechanical, electrical, and plumbing ducts.
For both bridges, Cimolai fabricated all the steel assemblies in its workshop in Italy.
The more complex parts as the arches were trialled first in Italy, and then shipped and installed by local subcontractors on site.
To facilitate the construction of all the bridges, the water was first pumped out of the canal, and temporary towers were used to support the structures during the operations and then removed before the water was allowed to flow back into the canal.
Local surveyors performed constant geometric controls during the pre-assembly phase of the parts on the ground, and also monitored the final installation. However, Cimolai engineers supervised the subcontractors' activities and coordinated the construction schedule with the other trades involved in the commission at each stage of execution, up until the final delivery to the client.

Dubai Parallel Roads

Company: Salini Impregilo (now Webuild)

Client: Roads and Transport Authority, Dubai (RTA)

Location: Dubai, UAE

Period of execution: 2007–2013

The project, named by MEED as the "United Arab Emirates Project of the Year"[1] in 2014 in the transport section, involved the construction of two important road sections in Dubai: the first near the World Trade Center connecting Second Zabeel Road to Sheikh Rashid Road; the second consisting of a series of roads and bridges to improve traffic flow in the Jumeirah Lake Towers area. In 2007 the project was awarded to Webuild as main contractor.

The construction of the 24 bridges stipulated by the two contractual lots represented the main challenge since they required special solutions, including the use of launching gantries with an innovative methodology for the first lot in order to finish the work quickly – and reduce traffic disruption.
The project also included the construction of new roads, the expansion of existing ones, the construction of access ramps and

Left and right: Aerial views of the parallel road section near the World Trade Center connecting Zabeel Road to Sheikh Zayed Road, 2013.

installation of vertical and horizontal signs, street lighting, and the repositioning of a high number of sub-services (electrical cables from 11 to 132 KV, telephone lines, internet lines, drainage, irrigation, and drinking water pipes up to a 1,200 mm in diameter).
The first contract included the construction of 17 bridges in precast segments with launching gantries for a total coverage of 60,000 sq.m and 6 pre-stressed concrete bridges cast in situ for a total of 7,200 sq.m of coverage. Both types reach spans up to 60 metres and have foundation piles with diameters of 1,000 or 2,000 mm. The second segment of the project involved the construction of 7 post-tensioned bridges cast in-situ, a 645-metre underpass and a pumping station, as well as other various construction activities such as road paving, signage, street lighting, traffic deviations, and the safeguard of existing services.
The precast bridges were created with launching gantries through the implementation of an innovative system known as "combo", which combines the "balanced cantilever" and "span-by-span" methods. The balanced cantilever method involves building a span starting with the launch of the two ends (above the piles) and completing the launch with the casting of the central segment. The combo method involves launching 5 segments on each pile and completing the span in a second phase by launching the remaining segments, as is normally done with the span-by-span method. This system allows the flexibility typical of the balanced cantilever method to be taken advantage of at the same time as the rapid launching in the span-by-span system (casting the central segment can be avoided in this manner).

[1] MEED March 2014.

Al Qassimi Women's and Children's Hospital and Emergency Department

Architecture Design: Urbanism Planning Architecture – UPA Consultancy & UPA Italia in partnership with General Planning

Healthcare Design and Medical Equipment: Progetto MCK

Surfaces Supplier Company: Fiandre Architectural Surfaces

Client: Ministry of Public Works UAE

Location: Sharjah, UAE

Period of execution: 2007–2014

Area: 61,000 sq.m (GFA), 43,500 sq.m (BuA)

The Al Qassimi Women's and Children's Hospital was developed by General Planning in a joint venture with UPA – Urbanism Planning Architecture and Progetto MCK, under the UAE Ministry of Public Works commission in 2007.[1] To the request to implement the existing services within the Al Qassimi Hospital, the client also demanded to expand the Women's and children's division by creating an emergency department. This A&E extension was created to link the new hospital complex with the existing one, and respond to the need for a more efficient emergency health service.
In detail, General Planning was appointed for the architecture and coordination, UPA as a consultant

Al Qassimi Hospital has a rational design: pure geometric volumes, perpendicular lines, and circle, 2014.

Opposite: Interior of the hospital's main hall, 2014. A wide window opens to the sandy exterior landscape, giving luminosity to the entrance and public space during the day. Sustainable materials were used for surfaces, such as the flooring with Active Surfaces, a photocatalytic material supplied by Fiandre Architectural Surfaces.

with UPA Italia for design and site supervision, and Progetto MCK for the consultancy services for medical planning and equipment. The architectural project is developed with rational space management that is physically translated with a clear separation between the various wards: the three main units (gynaecology, obstetrics, and paediatrics), the VIP and royal ward (six suites and three royal suites) with private entrance, areas for patients and areas dedicated to medical treatments. In the project, three parallel wings set orthogonally to the two main corridors define the three central units: the hospital circulation spine and the sanitary corridor. Each wing is functionally organized vertically, with outpatients at the main entrance facing the connectivity spine with upper-level wards.
The representative spaces, the main entrance, and the cafeteria are architecturally recognizable with volumes based on pure forms: the entrance is square, cafeteria circular, and the VIP wards are ellipses. The new A&E pavilion lies between the old section and the hospital extension, and links the two buildings.
The hospital has been designed as a modern machine with simple and functional forms. Based on the idea of light colours, the interior and exterior convey a sense of care and health, enhanced by the contrast with dark elements such as the window surfaces and the details on the flooring.
Importance has been given to the surrounding greenspace (gardens, fountains, courtyards) and natural light management. Large windows and skylights provide natural lighting and create a pleasant atmosphere for visiting patients, doctors, and relatives. The lanes oriented east to the west make the most of the sunlight, and render a more effective perception of the flow of time during the day.
Particular care has been paid to the patient areas. In the hospital rooms, the windows are set 60cm from the floor to allow the patient a more comprehensive view of the outside. In addition, the dark windows and the roller blinds are devised to offer optimal patient privacy. In all departments, the internal distribution of spaces is arranged to separate patient and visitor flows, guaranteeing privacy until the end of the treatment process.
The project follows the American Institute of Architects health services guidelines, and involves

the most modern technological equipment combining technical excellence and respect for the environment.
The design of all the medical equipment by General Planning with the consultancy of Progetto MCK is characterized by an eco-compatible approach geared to reducing energy consumption through non-renewable sources, and the emission of pollutants such as greenhouse gases. Additionally, high technological levels used in all the furnishings, medical equipment, safety, and communication, determine an authentic humanization of services to ensure comfort and reduce the need for intervention by the auxiliary staff.
Attention has also been paid to the choice of materials that define the functional needs of the environment.
The internal flooring of the common areas consists of a seamless white surface alternated with black stripes, creating a geometrical pattern. This flooring material is called ACTIVE SURFACES®, and offers a 100% Italian-made high-performance ceramic surface, supplied by the Italian company Fiandre Architectural Surfaces. Thanks to a particular treatment, Active Surfaces help eliminate pollutants and microbial agents (viruses, bacteria, fungi, and moulds) and unpleasant odours, ensuring a hygienic and healthier environment fundamental for healthcare facilities.
This ceramic surface is the product of extensive and innovative research conducted by the company for advanced solutions that combine aesthetics with functionality, aiming to improve the quality of life.
The Italian touch is also present in the furniture of the entire hospital, and in the lighting.

[1] In 2007 the Minister of the Infrastructure of Abu Dhabi wanted to develop two hospitals, one in the Emirate of Sharjah and the other one in the Emirate of Ajman. The concept for both hospitals was proposed by General Planning in partnership with UPA for the design phase, who then acquired the contract for the project and construction of Al Qassimi Hospital in Sharjah and Masfout Hospital in Ajman (2007–2011). A twin of the Masfout Hospital was later built under the supervision of UPA in the Emirate of Ras Al Khaimah (2011–2019).

Al Qassimi Hospital, 2014. The light hues of the building surfaces create striking contrasts with the black glazing.

Mangrove Place

Architecture Design: Urbanism Planning Architecture – UPA Consultancy & UPA Italia

Client: Luxury Real Estate Development

Location: Abu Dhabi, UAE

Period of Execution: 2007–2014

Area: about 80,000 sq.m

Mangrove Place is a residential tower overlooking the Mangrove Canal on Al Reem Island. The area is considered one of the most rapidly developing neighbourhoods In Abu Dhabi.
Designed by Aswan Ibrahim Zubaidi and Paolo Lettieri, the building is characterized by staggered terraces and balconies that offer a panoramic sea view. The distinctive form visually contrasts with the glass skyscrapers that surround the area, breaking the rhythm of vertical blocks.
The pattern of stepped terraces and the generosity of its space also contribute to reducing the sense of vertigo that occurs on towers of this height, and gives the apartments excellent headroom liveability.
After developing the final project and tendering it out to the constructor, UPA was subsequently called in to redefine the executive project.
In addition, the architects developed the interior design of the common parts and intervened in the façades, which were considerably modified during construction. The shape of the windows was redefined vertically, creating an asymmetrical pattern in order to break the monotony of the lateral façades, since it was not possible to change the percentage of glass, which had already been contractually defined between the builder and the owner company.
The resulting façades are entirely clad in stone, with a finished split stone to define the string courses and play off against the vertical window arrays.
The building is distributed over 29 storeys, of which two comprise the podium, plus three levels of underground parking that hold up to 600 vehicles; the tower offers 481 apartments and duplexes of various dimensions, commercial spaces, public facilities – such as a swimming pool and gymnasium – covering a total area of around 80,000 square metres.

Overlooking the Mangrove Canal, the terraced structure of Mangrove Place contrast with the skyscraper in the background, 2021.

Al Maharat Private School

Architecture Design: M+N Architecture

Client: KHX Education

Main Contractor: Genesis Manazil

Location: Shakhbout City, Abu Dhabi, UAE

Period of execution: 2014–2015

Area: 16,625 sq.m

In 2013 M+N Architecture, an Italian firm specialized in the design of educational buildings, was called in by KHX Education for the design and development of Al Maharat Private School, an educational complex implementing the Arabic curriculum (Abu Dhabi Ministry of Education Curriculum).

Set to accommodate around 2,000 students from kindergarten to grade 12, the project spreads over three levels, and comprises seventy-six classrooms, several science labs, an art room, a music room, a library, a gym/multipurpose hall, indoor and outdoor play areas, and assorted other facilities.

The school is designed according to the standards set out by ADEC (Abu Dhabi Education Council) and provides gender-segregated spaces from grade five and above, as per Arabic curriculum school standards.

The building has five separate accesses to allow the flow of different age groups, and a complex internal connectivity to comply with several segregation and security requirements.

The main corridors and the shared facilities are conceived as a central service spine along which different clusters of classrooms are attached perpendicularly as "wings" and complemented by a "head" (the main reception, library, and kindergarten) and a "tail" (gym/multipurpose hall).

The main volumes at the two ends of the building provide most of its architectural character.

A prominent mass with two inclined elevations and asymmetrical windows marks the school's main entrance and hosts the library. The gym/multipurpose hall is a simple "box" with two sets of staggered vertical windows.
The kindergarten is a ground-only volume with huge colourful skylights shaped like truncated pyramids visible from outside. It features an impressive 627 sq.m indoor breakout/play area surrounded by eight kindergarten classrooms featuring six large and colourful skylights that allow natural light to flood the space, creating a natural but protected environment for teaching, play, and socialization.
The classroom arrangement around this central social space creates a sense of community and a significant level of interaction amongst the kids, increasing shared learning between different age groups. Each classroom is provided with fully openable glass partitions on the side of the indoor breakout area and characterized by tetromino windows facing an outdoor playground.
The interiors have been conceived to be practical, flexible, and allow natural light throughout the building. Internal courtyards have been designed along the central spine, providing access and views to the outside from the corridors and special rooms. A different design and colour of the finishes of the internal aisles characterize the three different educational cycles in the building.
Double-height voids emphasize the internal spaces in the library and

View of the south-east and north-east façades. The architecture stands out from its sandy surroundings.

Opposite: View of Al Maharat Private school's main entrance and library on the right side with asymmetrical windows, 2016.

the main open staircase in front of the main entrance.

In conformance with ADEC design guidelines and Estidama requirements (the Abu Dhabi regulation for sustainable construction), 50% of the external play areas are covered with shading structures or canopies to protect children from direct exposure to the sun. Additionally, roof gardens are implemented to be used as outdoor learning and breakout spaces for older students to cope with a shortage of outdoor space, given the limited size of the plot.

The Al Maharat Private School is the first large educational structure to be built using a prefabricated system based on cold-formed galvanized steel panels produced in a factory environment by computer-controlled machines and then installed on-site in eighteen months. Only the stairs, the elevator cores and the foundations are in reinforced concrete.

The kindergarten has a main load-bearing structure in hot-rolled engineered steel cladded with magnesium oxide boards completely water-resistant and a double insulation layer that gives the school excellent thermal insulation coefficients.

In 2015 the school was shortlisted for the category "Green School of the Year" at the Emirates Green Building Council Award in Dubai.

South-west view of the building façade.

Left: The skylights flood the kindergarten area with natural light.

Dubai Water Canal – Footbridges

Companies: Swissboring (Trevi Group), Maeg Costruzioni, Redaelli Tecna

Architecture Design: Parsons Overseas Limited / Halcrow International Partnership

Client: Joint Venture Road and Transport Authority (RTA), Meydan and Meraas

Main Contractor: Belhasa Six Construct LLC (BESIX)

Location: Dubai, UAE

Period of execution: 2014–2016

Area: 3.2 sq.km

The second footbridge named the "Tolerance Bridge" in honour of the International Day of Tolerance, 2016.

Opposite: The first footbridge, also known as Safa Bridge, 2016

One of Dubai's most significant urban transformation projects is the so-called artificial Dubai Water Canal.
Conceived as a new, fully navigable route, the waterway extension covers 3.2 kilometres with a 6.4-km-long waterfront project. Starting from Deira Creek in the city's Old Quarter, the canal passes through Business Bay, the main road artery known as Sheikh Zayed Road, stretches to Safa Park, Jumeirah, and ends in the Arabian Gulf.
The canal, designed to be a waterfront destination estimated to attract 30 million visitors per year, opens up to a new vibrant hub for residential, commercial, hotels, and retail and offers a luxury canal living and stunning views in the three main areas: Safa, Jumeirah, and Peninsula.[1] In this way, the development will enhance the tourist and commercial activities along the banks as well as the surrounding area.[2]
The entire project also comprises the construction of nine water taxis, along with five bridges to develop and manage integrated and sustainable roads and transportation systems at a world-class level.
Furthermore, three footbridges link both sides of the canal with unique aesthetic specifications echoing Dubai's history, present, and future with their architecture. This new concept of shorefront development reveals the importance of the presence of the water not only as a landscape feature, but ideologically connecting the past of the city to its modern urban evolving transformation, contributing to creating a sense of place and identity.[3]

The canal is a project that accentuates Dubai's city image as an urban space founded upon technologically advanced infrastructural systems offering new panoramas of the city to improve the quality of life.
The worldwide team of companies involved in developing this contemporary architectural-engineering masterpiece saw the contributions of several Italian companies.
In its field, Swissboring (Trevi Group) was commissioned in 2014 for the canal excavation and the foundation services with the application of 136 bored piles (ø1,000 and ø1,200). This technology is used to stabilize the terrain through the process called desanding. Its purpose is to reduce the size of the site and minimize soil debris that is polluted by stabilizing slurries. In this way, the mud is regenerated by removing the coarsest material of the soil.[4]
The work carried out by Swissboring (Trevi Group) involved not only the drilling and the constructing sides of the water canal: in addition, it has also been involved in the construction of four marine transit stations to boost the role of maritime transport, and the three footbridges linking the two banks of the channel.
Each footbridge has a distinct structural form. There is a grand arch that is all curves, a low-slung suspension bridge, and a twisted truss. Although each of the bridges looks very different in design at first sight, they are made with steel as primary construction materials. Therefore, two major Italian companies in the steel industries were chosen for their construction.
In May 2016 Maeg Costruzioni won the tender as a subcontractor of the main contractor Belhasa Six Construct, the Dubai-based entity of BESIX. For its expertise, Maeg Costruzioni was in charge of the design, fabrication, and installation of steel structures, while Redaelli supplied and installed cable systems for two of the three pedestrian bridges.
The Dubai Water Canal was a challenging project within a highly tight design and construction plan. Despite all challenges derived from the several requirements, the overall project succeeded, and the companies accomplished all technical and timing demands.
On 9 November 2016 the Dubai Water Canal was officially inaugurated and opened to the public.

Footbridge 01

The first footbridge crossing the Dubai Water Canal, also called the Safa bridge, connects the Al Wasl district to Safa Park, one of the city's principal green spaces. Its design was inspired by the Arab nomadic culture of trade and fishing history, the Y-shaped masts and suspension cables of the footbridge reminiscent of Bedouin tent design. The metal structure is suspended by steel cables at a height of 8.5 metres above the water level to allow navigation space along the canal. It is supported by the particular design of two Y-shaped pylons weighing 90 tons each and 35 metres high that were installed inside the channel before it was re-flooded with water. The bridge's deck is 122 metres long, 6.2 metres wide, and was dispatched from the Maeg's factory in eleven segments,

then installed on temporary towers, and then completed with the welding.
The structure can support its weight thanks to 252 metres of steel cables, on which are anchored hanger rods with an inclined configuration of 45 degrees that gives the particular catenary effect. Redaelli supplied back span and main span full locked coil cables and rod system for the hangers. Cables were manufactured with a high-quality prefabricated system, produced under factory-controlled conditions, which guarantee the strict tolerance required by the coupling with spherical bearings so as to permit possible adjustment in the alignments of the structures. On-site tensioning was performed with all cables installed and structures placed on temporary supports. Throughout the tensioning process, the geometry of the footbridge was strictly monitored to verify that the actual displacements of the structure comply with the designer tensioning procedure. Only after the installation and tensioning of the steel cables was it possible to remove the temporary towers.

Footbridge 02

The second bridge is located between Sheikh Zayed Road and Al Wasl Road. This structure reflects Dubai's interwoven cultural connections. His Highness Sheikh Mohammed bin Rashid Al Maktoum, the Vice-President and Prime Minister of the United Arab Emirates and Governor of Dubai, has renamed the project "Bridge of Tolerance", symbolizing the connection between the different cultures and nationalities present in the city.[5]
This footbridge is characterized by an arched structure having a width of 205 metres and a height of 50. The S-shape of the deck is a cross-section of 6 metres at the base tapers up to 2.1 in the critical section, giving a sense of lightness and fluidity. Maeg Costruzioni pre-assembled the arch and welded it to the ground in nine macro-segments that were subsequently hoisted to the top of temporary towers, reaching their tallest point at 53 metres, through two 600-ton crawler cranes. The weight of the arch alone is 1,700 tons and, through 20 steel cables (for a total length of 858 metres), supports the distinctive S-shaped design deck, curling in two concrete ramps wrapped around the bases of the arch gently above the water.
All the arch cables are anchored to the centreline at the topside, whereas the bottom anchorages are located on the left side of the deck for the first half of its length, and to the right side for the other half. All cables were installed in two months, and the tensioning of all the hangers was carried out in a single night by Redaelli.

Footbridge 03

The third footbridge crossing the Dubai Water Canal is a marvel of engineering, pointing to the future of Dubai and its dynamic vision. It is a parallelepiped twisting 180 degrees, wrapping around the internal walkway and offering a dynamic movement accompanying those who pass through it. The footbridge is clad with a series of aluminium frames protecting from the sun from an oblique angle but allowing an open view towards the city skyline when passing through. The construction phase took place during one of the most critical moments, just before the scheduled flooding of the canal on the inauguration date. This condition prevented working directly from inside the channel, forcing the installation to be completed just over a month. The solution adopted by Maeg Costruzioni was to install a temporary bridge that supported preassembled elements until welding was completed, thereby ensuring a working surface on which to operate, which was then removed. The temporary bridge was tethered to a barge which, taking advantage of the low tide, was freed from the permanent structure and then transported somewhere else to be dismantled separately.
The footbridge measures 6.5x6.5 metres and has a total weight of 1,386 tons. Called Jumeirah Bridge 2, the structure connects the district of Al Safa to the archaeological site of Jumeirah.

[1] DWC Brochure: www.meeras.com.
[2] T. KT (9 November 2016), "Dubai Water Canal: All that you need to know", *Khaleej Times*: https://www.khaleejtimes.com/nation/dubai/dubai-water-canal-all-that-you-need-to-know (accessed 27 June 2021).
[3] M. El Amrousi, M. ElHakeem, E. Paleologos, and M.A. Misuri, "Engineered landscapes: The New Dubai Canal and emerging public spaces", *International Review for Spatial Planning and Sustainable Development*, 7, 3 (2019): 33–44.
[4] https://www.swissboring.com/Technologies/bored_piles. In the Gulf architecture, traditional motifs with functional goals merge and are used often in order to shape regional cultural identity and the foundation for new transnational formations. To examine in more depth the identity discourse in the Gulf, is suggested the reading of the essay by Amale Andros "Problematizing a Regional context in H. Molotch and D. Ponzini" (eds.), *The New Arab Urban: Gulf Cities of Wealth, Ambition, and Distress* (NYU Press, 2019), pp. 58–78.
[5] A. Zacharias (15 November 2017), "Sheikh Mohammed names pedestrian bridge over Dubai Canal ‚Tolerance Bridge", *The National*. https://www.thenationalnews.com/uae/sheikh-mohammed-names-pedestrian-bridge-_over-dubai-canal-tolerance-bridge-1.676094 (accessed 12 September 2021).

The third footbridge, with its unusual twisted form.

Palazzo Versace

Architecture and Interior Design: SPATIUM

Companies: Fantini Mosaici, Swissboring (Trevi Group), Prysmian Group

Client: Versace; Enshaa PSC

Contractor: Emirates Sunland Group, under a joint venture with Arabtec

Location: Al Jaddaf Waterfront, Dubai, UAE

Period of Execution: 2007–2015; opened in 2016

Palazzo Versace in Dubai, the second of the brand's boutique hospitality venues worldwide,[1] is a luxury five-star hotel and residential resort located on the banks of the historic Dubai Creek.
Designed by the Italian architecture firm SPATIUM (Lorenzo Carmellini and Rocco Magnoli),[2] in charge of both the architecture and the interior design, the hotel's neo-Classical architecture is inspired by the typical sixteenth-century Italian Palazzo, and contains 215 individual rooms and suites, and 169 residences called the Condominium.
The name Palazzo for the Versace hotel is a tribute to Gianni Versace's love for Classical architecture (European, and especially Italian).
It is characterized by the exquisite proportion of the parts to each other and to the whole, informing regularity and brightness to the interior spaces, and guaranteeing the richness of design in the decorations, the relationship with the garden and the landscape, transforming a civic building into a palace.
The Palazzo Versace rises from a protruding platform as the fortification of a citadel surrounded by water, and offers an unobstructed view of the Dubai Creek and skyline.
It is symmetrically divided into a central body twelve floors high, with two rear concave wings of eleven storeys, all rising from a tall arcade, which is also concave and extends to its maximum width to accommodate and define the hotel's entrance.

Opposite: Palazzo Versace, entrance façade (opposite) by SPATIUM, 2017.

Top right: The Medusa, the symbol of the Italian fashion designer Versace, is detailed reproduced on the Hotel Lobby floor in marble by Fantini Mosaici.

Below: The furniture and the fabrics adorning all the hotel rooms were designed by the Maison Versace exclusively for the Palazzo Versace in Dubai.

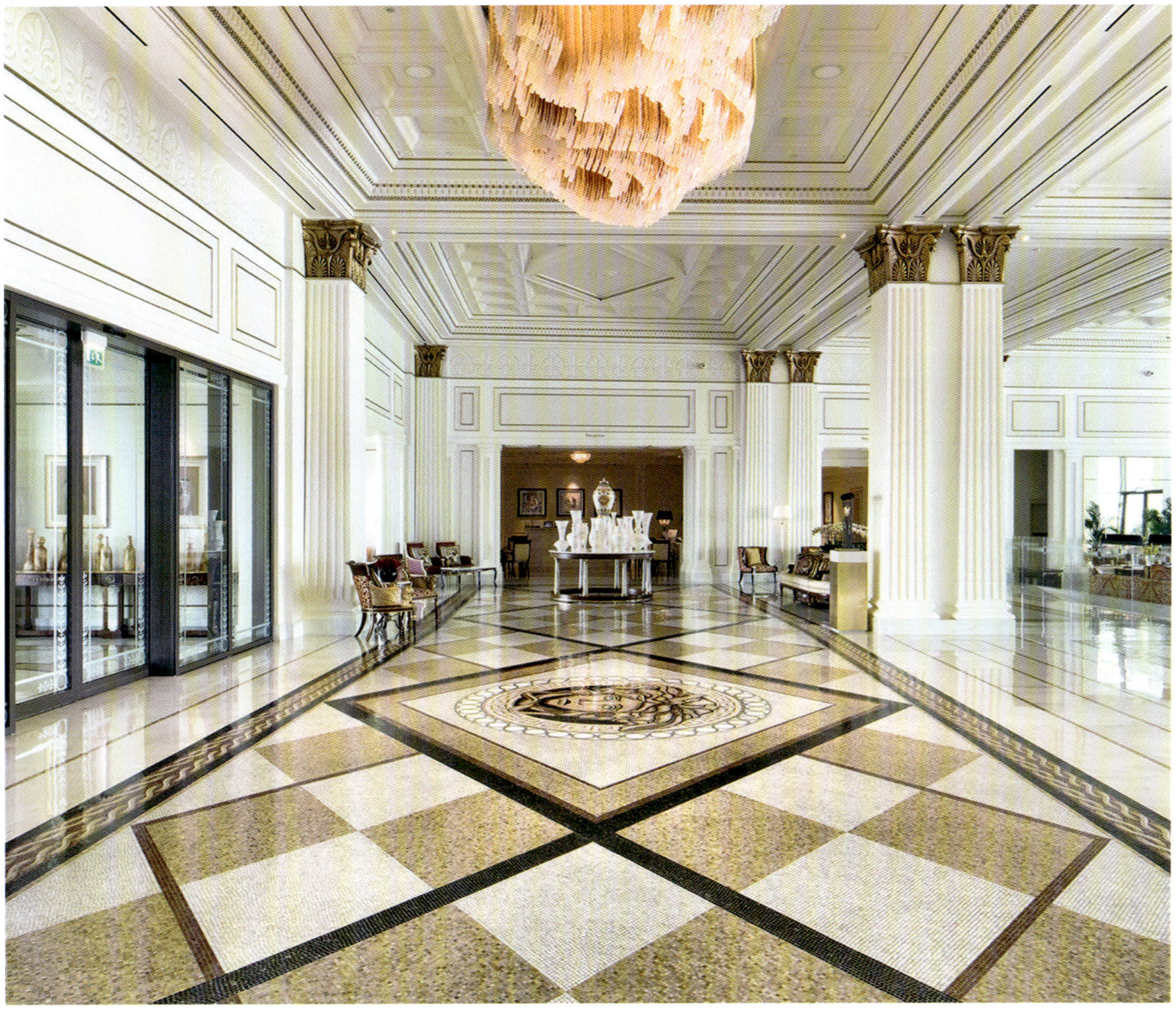

Two large ten-storey pavilions project orthogonally from the main body, oriented towards the Creek to optimize the view of each housing unit.
The Classical architecture inspires the design of the Palazzo: a strong base on which rests a body marked by pillars following a rhythm that balances the width with the height, concluded by a crowning element which in turn is subdivided into three parts: architrave, frieze, and cornice. In this way, the large complex is re-proportioned, articulated in protrusions both in plan and in elevation, enhanced with different types of roofing to avoid repetition and visually reduce its bulk. Classical design characterizes the exterior of the buildings, such as in the façade, which protrudes from the walls of the rooms to contain the terraces without accentuating the horizontal lines. The style is interwoven with subtle traces of Arabian architecture, such as the openwork connecting the pillars, shielding the interiors from excessive light. Different cultures designed the protection of buildings from sunlight in different ways, dividing the views from the inside as images in a kaleidoscope.
The interiors evince the cross-pollination of styles and the depth of cultural references on which Versace's later ideas are based: the historical references (neo-Baroque and neo-Classical) are counterpointed by modern and contemporary idioms. Every single item of furniture and all the details of the fabrics that adorn the hotel rooms and suites are designed and tailor-made by Versace.
The venue is a masterpiece that combines Italian craftsmanship and the elegance of a fashion-branded space.
For Palazzo Versace, the Italian mosaic company Fantini Mosaici supplied and installed over 70,000 sq.m of marble inserts hand-cut to size, comprising mosaics, patterned terrazzo flooring, and external pebble-stone paving.[3]
Beautifully detailed mosaics and intricately patterned stonework grace the hotel driveway, adorn the common area floors and walls, the spa and private residences, the bathrooms and swimming pools. Everywhere one can see the motifs of the Medusa and the Greek

Palace interior view. The neo-Classical architecture of the interiors is expressed through the harmonic proportions of the space, the use of Corinthian columns, and the ceiling decorated with linear motifs and bas-relief. The entire area is articulated by the use of different motifs in the marble flooring.

Marble carpet by Fantini Mosaici reproducing in *tromp-l'œil* Versace's signature silk scarf.

fretwork pattern. A particularly iconic piece is found in the lobby: the mosaic flooring is a trompe-l'oeil inspired by Giovanni Versace's hallmark silk scarf with Baroque motifs in gold. This glorious *oeuvre* is composed of over one million hand-cut tesserae, each one manually set in place.
When construction works started in 2009 two major Italian companies were involved: Swissboring (Trevi Group) – a worldwide leader in the field of soil engineering – was appointed in 2007 for the piling and shoring of the Palazzo's foundations, which required main piles of different diameters, secant piles with tie-back anchors, and contiguous piles; in addition, the Milan-based Prysmian Group – a global leader in the energy and telecom cable systems industry – provided hundreds of kilometres of standard and enhanced fire-resistant cable able to guarantee the supply of energy and the smooth functioning of the security signalling system, even in the event of a fire.
After eight years of work, the Palazzo Versace officially opened in November 2016.

[1] The first Versace hotel opened on the Gold Coast in Australia was the pioneer of fashion-luxury hotels. https://www.versace.com/it/it-it/palazzo-versace/.
[2] In 1979 the architecture studio SPATIUM – Lorenzo Carmellini and Rocco Magnoli – created the image for the Versace boutiques around the world. It was the beginning of a twenty-year collaboration that led to designing all the flagship stores and more than 300 boutiques and corners worldwide. Further to the experience gained in the fashion industry, the subsequent step was to get involved in the tourist-hotel industry. In 1998 Carmellini and Magnoli were commissioned to design the overall image of the first Versace hotel: Palazzo Versace in Gold Coast, Australia (2001) and then in Dubai in 2018.
[3] It is worth mentioning that Fantini Mosaici also supplied and installed the mosaics for the first Versace Hotel in Gold Coast, Queensland (Australia).

Qasr Al Watan

Company: Fantini Mosaici

Client: Ministry of Presidential Affairs (MOPA)

Location: Al Ras Al Akhdar, Abu Dhabi, UAE

Period of execution: 2010–2017

Area: 380,000 sq.m

Qasr Al Watan is the Presidential palace of the United Arab Emirates. Translated from Arabic as the "Place of the Nation", it is "a unique cultural landmark, a place that looks to the future, drawing inspiration from the past".[1] A place open to the entire world, and which invites people to discover and admire the rich Arab heritage, artistry, and knowledge that have shaped the history of the UAE.[2]
Qasr Al Watan was built for merely the official purpose of state visits and summits.
It took seven years – from 2010 to 2017 – to finish the construction of the 380,000 sq.m citadel. On 11 March 2019 the palace opened a dedicated section – the main building – to the public to explore its beauty and a vast collection of artefacts and manuscripts.[3] The Presidential complex also houses the offices of the President, Vice-President, and Crown Prince. These three buildings are situated at the rear of the main building.
A jewel of the Arabian Peninsula, the architecture of the Palace takes its inspiration from the style of the Mughal era, juxtaposing the traditional architecture and artistic legacy of the Arab region, such as archways, domes, lush gardens, and fountains, precious ornaments, and mosaic patterns.

The marina and the sea surround the Presidential Palace, like a citadel. Entirely clad in white granite and limestone, it gleams during the day.

Opposite: Close-up of the domes crowning the main entrance of the Presidential Palace. Design and decorated by Fantini Mosaici, with curvilinear motifs in glass and gold mosaics.

Following the rules of symmetry, the architectural features are geometrically and mathematically proportional. In elevation, the walls are covered with marble and mosaics. Slabs of marble are placed side by side with a book-matched technique.

Opposite top right: View of the Palace Great Hall, the largest space in Qasr Al Watan, used for important celebrations.

Opposite bottom: The mosaics by Fantini Mosaici feature several patterns in the 14th- and 15th-century Moroccan style. In the shades of blue, azure, brown, and gold, the colourful mosaics offset the pale glow of the marble.

The monumental Palace is enveloped in white granite and limestone, making it glow during the day, when the sun burnishes the façade. The white surfaces reflect the theme of peace and prosperity, which are also conveyed in the hues of the interiors design.

The over 112 domes that crown the buildings were designed and built by the Italian mosaic firm Fantini Mosaici, with sinuous curvilinear organic-geometric forms the employ a mixture of enamel, plus 18,000 sq.m of glass mosaics, including myriad silver and 24-carat gold tesserae.

Crowning the main building is a single giant dome, one of the largest in the world, with a diameter of 37 metres and depth of 15. The dome rises above the Great Hall, a vast space measuring 100 metres by 100, the structure's heart, as it is used for important ceremonies and cultural celebrations.

The stunning interiors follow the demands of symmetry: the building's geometrically and mathematically proportional features were completed by Fantini Mosaici, employing marble and 6,000 sq.m of mosaics. Beautiful and intricate floral and geometric mosaics patterns in enamel, marble, precious stone (mother of pearl, lapis lazuli, malachite) and gold handcrafted by Fantini Mosaici adorn the walls, ceiling, and internal surfaces of the domes. The mosaics are inspired by Islamic art and feature several patterns influenced by the Moroccan style of the 14th and 15th centuries.

Throughout Qasr Al Watan, marble is a key element: the floors are all paved with waterjet marble, and marble slabs clad the walls, creating

a distinctive design known as the book-matched marble technique. With the mosaics, marble creates a colour gradient effect. The light palette used throughout the Palace interiors was specifically chosen by H.H. Sheikh Khalifa bin Zayed Al Nayan. White, pale blue, azure, and brown are the primary colours that unify the Palace's surface palette and overall design, and represent the essence of the UAE culture: white symbolizes purity and peace, azure the sky, blue the Arabian gulf, and brown the desert. The space of the Great Hall is impressive and can be explored thanks to mirror cube installations that emphasize the architectural details and ornamentation, allowing visitors to explore the design elements further.
The east wing houses the library with its "incredible collection of timeless literature".[4] While the west wing is home to the *majlis*, where important meetings are hosted for the Federal Supreme Council, the Arab League, and the Gulf Cooperation Council.

[1] From an advertisment of Qasr Al Watan.
[2] Qasr Al Watan official website. www.qasral-watan.ae.
[3] "Abu Dhabi Presidential Palace to open its doors to the public" (5 March 2019), *The National*. https://www.thenationalnews.com/uae/heritage/abu-dhabi-presidential-palace-to-open-its-doors-to-the-public-1.832921 (accessed 15 November 2021).
[4] https://www.qasralwatan.ae/en/explore-the-palace/qasr-al-watan-library (accessed 10 November 2021).

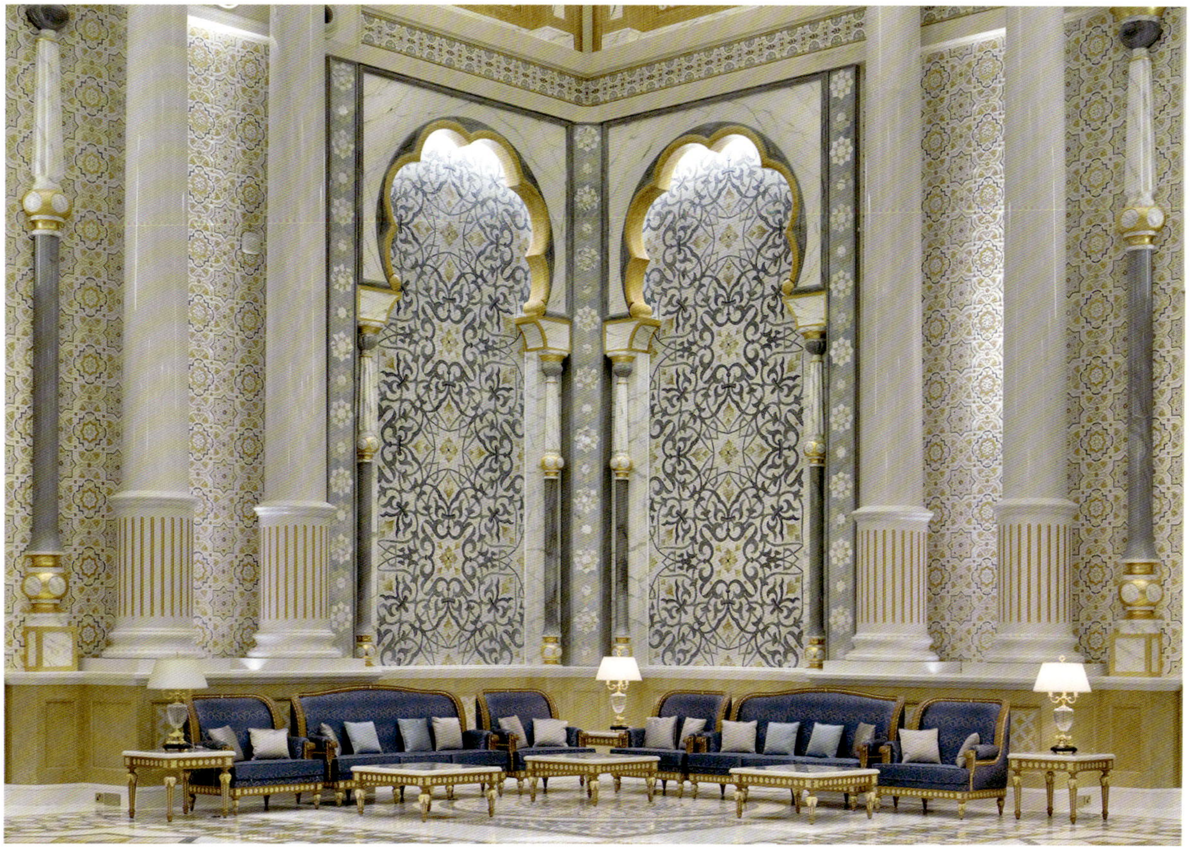

Louvre Abu Dhabi

Companies: Artemide, Mapei, Nesite, Poltrona Frau, Prysmian Group, Savema

Architecture Design: Ateliers Jean Nouvel

Client: Department of Culture and Tourism - Abu Dhabi (DCT Abu Dhabi)

Location: Saadiyat Island, Abu Dhabi, UAE

Period of execution: 2006–2017

Area: 97,000 sq.m

The Louvre Abu Dhabi is a "universal museum", an encounter between different cultures and people.[1]
Born from an unprecedented partnership between the governments of France and Abu Dhabi signed in March 2007, the Louvre Abu Dhabi opened its doors in the Cultural District of Saadiyat Island in November 2017.
Rising from the sea, the complex designed by Jean Nouvel, 2008 laureate of the Pritzker Architecture Prize, comprises a lavish, silver-plated dome that sprawls over a conglomeration of white cubic volumes.
Taking inspiration from the region's traditional *medina*, the design is a marvellous "synthesis of the traditional and modern in the Gulf."[2]
The centrepiece of Nouvel's vision is the dome itself. The fulcrum of the building, the dome consists of a complex perforated geometric 180-metre structure that filters the sun rays, creating a "rain of light" effect on the semi-open plaza beneath, generating a magical and immaterial atmosphere that

constantly changes according the sun's position in the sky.
Light is an essential architectural element for Nouvel.[3] He readily plays with light and shadow to create a uniquely fluid spatial narrative. Nouvel's attention to this element in shaping the architecture matches Artemide's deep knowledge and ongoing commitment to lighting design. The consideration that Jean Nouvel and Artemide have been conducting for some time emerged in fruitful collaboration and experimentation for Louvre Abu Dhabi. The result led to a new version of the Cata light projection system.
Designed by Carlotta de Bevilacqua, Cata Tir adjusts to the continuous changes of natural light that filters through Nouvel's huge floating dome, providing flexible, controlled, and specific illumination of works of different dimensions and materials, ages, and styles. Each appliance is set to a specific light level, which adjust as the natural light conditions change, each one specific to the work on display and the shifting lightscape inside the museum.
This rich performance is transposed into an appliance based on the principles of transparency and lightness. Its presence in space is thus dematerialized, granting the leading role to light.
Artemide was also appointed to illuminate the exhibiting museum rooms and the public shopping areas, with catadioptric versions of the Cata projector. Service areas are fitted with appliances from the design collection, including Dioscuri; whereas the iconic functional Tolomeo units provide all the office illumination.

Opposite: Louvre Abu Dhabi, Atelier Jean Nouvel, 2017. The museum rises from the sea of the Saadiyat Cultural District, an ambitious development conceived to become a global hub for art, culture, and tourism, hosting world-class exhibitions. The Louvre Abu Dhabi is the first museum to be completed on the island.

Below: Many parts of the museum are immersed in water, which presented various challenges in terms of the choice of materials applied by Mapei.

The flooring beneath the dome is paved with Pietra di Luserna supplied by Savema, a resistant shiny grey material. During the day, the dome roof filters the natural light creating a shifting "rain of light" that pervades the space with constantly changing contrasts dancing across all the surfaces.

At the Louvre Abu Dhabi, every element contributes to the character of the building, such as the flooring, which differs in each area according to function. Parts of the interior and exterior paving of the public concourses are covered with Italian Pietra di Luserna, supplied by the Savema company based in Pietrasanta, Italy. It was the architect himself who selected the material he felt most appropriate. Working alongside Nouvel in the preparation of the material, Savema provided over 30,000 sq.m of this grey stone, a material with plenty of history behind it and many noble uses in the past.
The flooring of the interior permanent exhibition galleries is covered with marble of different types, contributing to differentiate each gallery and at the same time presenting "an individual appearance, and atmosphere".[4]
Thanks to its expertise, Nesite has contributed to the completion of the Louvre in Abu Dhabi by installing over 20,000 sq.m of raised floor suitable for museum applications, with high mechanical (Class 5) and seismic (Eurocode and UBS) characteristics. The complexity of the project was further enhanced by the high level of product customization, which included the supply of special formats with various prestigious marble and natural stone coverings as Red Levanto, Baolite, Marquina, Black Saint Laurent, Blue du Hainaut, Black and dark Omani.
The installation of marble in the other parts of the museum was carried on using Mapei adhesives. It worked closely with the main marble subcontractor to achieve the high-quality finish requested, using specific products to meet the requirements of each area according to the type of marble, the substrate, and the ambient conditions.
One of the biggest challenges for the applicators was installing marble in a vast space with both dry and wet areas.
The marble slabs were installed on various complex substrates as precast concrete elements, steel and glass panels. Furthermore, certain areas were prone to large deformations, whereas, in other areas, the marble had to be installed on surfaces that were then to be immersed in the water. For such areas Mapei's technical service team conducted inspections of the substrate conditions prior to the application as well as specific training and advice regarding application techniques.
The beauty and essence of Louvre Abu Dhabi are intrinsic in all the single parts of the museum.

As Nouvel said, "architecture does not stop at the front door. Any detail has the potential to disrupt the sense of harmony and destroy meaning".[5]

Nouvel designed for the museum seats and furnishing elements working closely with the Italian Poltrona Frau. With its deeply Italian tradition yet one that is open to the world characterized by its solid creativity, strong research, and savoir-faire, the Italian brand becomes the privileged interlocutor capable of giving shape to the most daring ideas and requirements. Poltrona Frau Custom Interiors department team combined all its skills to work alongside Jean Nouvel, providing proactive support from the initial creative stages through to the completion of the project.

The results were 660 pieces designed and tailor-made.

The furniture collection includes double-sided black leather sofa benches, armchairs, stools, tables for the museum and gel-coated tables and benches for the Louvre Abu Dhabi café and restaurant. Simplicity and curvilinear forms are the main distinctive character that emphasizes the building scale and lines of composition fitting the environment perfectly.

The Louvre Abu Dhabi is surely one of the most cutting-edge and technically challenging projects realized in the capital for many years. The project involved the contribution of numerous companies during its construction. A particular marine work has been conducted by Prysmian Group which supplied and installed 500 km of fire-resistant cables, to ensure maximum safety for visitors and the masterpieces that are kept there.

[1] To know more about the museum philosophy, J.F. Charnier (ed.), *Louvre Abu Dhabi: The Complete Guide*, Skira, 2018.

[2] A. Andraos, "Problematizing a Regional Context: Representation in Arab and Gulf Cities", in *The New Arab Urban*. New York University Press, 2019, p. 62. For the French architect it was essential to sculpt a space pertinent to the historical culture of its context and environment. "Architecture has to be connected to the spirit of the place," he observed in an interview published in *The Art Newspaper*. V. Noce, "Exclusive interview with Jean Nouvel, architect of Louvre Abu Dhabi's wondrous building", *The Art Newspaper*, 6 September 2017. https://www.theartnewspaper.com/2017/09/06/exclusive-interview-with-jean-nouvel-architect-of-louvre-abu-dhabis-wondrous-building

[3] C.L. Morgan , J. Nouvel, *Jean Nouvel: the elements of architecture,* New York: Universe, 1998.

[4] Nouvel, J. (2018), Louvre Abu Dhabi: The Story of An Architectural Project, Paris edition, Skira (p. 62).

[5] Nouvel, J. (2018), *Louvre Abu Dhabi: The Story of An Architectural Project,* Paris edition, Skira (pp. 100–1).

Interior of the Modern wing, 2017. The area is illuminated by the Artemide technology of a Cata projector designed by Carlotta de Bevilacqua. The black leather sofa-bench is by Poltrona Frau, while the stone raised flooring is supplied and installed by Nesite.

BULGARI Resort

Architecture and Interior Design: ACPV ARCHITECTS Antonio Citterio Patricia Viel

Client: Meraas Development

Location: Jumeirah Bay Island, Dubai, UAE

Period of execution: 2013–2015 (design), 2016–2017 (construction)

Area: 130,000 sq.m (GFA); 123,000 sq.m (BuA)

The Bulgari Resort in Dubai is situated on the artificial Jumeirah Bay Island, an urban oasis and a highly sought-after destination forged in the shape of a giant seahorse[1].
Renowned Italian architectural firm ACPV ARCHITECTS Antonio Citterio Patricia Viel – which has created all the Bulgari hotels and resorts to date – designed the masterplan (architecture and interiors) of the Bulgari Resort Dubai with a purely Italian style. Inspired by the typical Mediterranean village, and crafting the property like a fine jewel, the architects chose rare, raw materials according to their colour, texture, and feel – creating a peerless example of luxury hospitality.

The 1.4 million-square-foot resort is a first-of-its-kind development for Bulgari, both in terms of scale and magnitude. The island property blends traditional Italian design with contemporary architecture embellished by Middle Eastern touches with its Mediterranean village charm and gardens.
The resort comprises the hotel building and the yacht-club pavilion located on the marina promenade. Meanwhile, situated on the shoreline, the Bulgari Villas offer a unique experience among the fragrant gardens of their private courtyards, the deep beachfront, and the city's spectacular skyline.

The exterior of the BULGARI Resort is designed on the overlay of horizontal lines with the podium in white veined Arabescato marble from Carrara, Italy. It is located on a man-made island with a sleek profile of a "seahorse": defining the arcs of sand and rocks.

Opposite: The façade is defined by the coral texture of the sunscreen that characterizes the two main buildings of the hotel.

The modern and minimalistic architecture of the hotel is staggered and articulated to match the profile of the promontory, which stretches out towards the horizon.

Opposite bottom right: Interior view of the hotel, with its surfaces in fine oak applied in long thin planks recalling the decks of a ship. All the furniture and interiors in the public areas and rooms are by the finest Italian brands, such as Maxalto, Flos, Flexform, and B&B Italia.

A merger of the goldsmith's art and sophisticated natural creation, the coral texture characterizes the two main buildings of the hotel. Based on an overlay of horizontal lines, the building façades are defined by the lively shadow pattern of coral-like sunscreens, though not to be confused with walls of the hotel podium, with its white marble richly veined with black and gold arabesques.
Surfaces of fine oak wood in long and thin planks – recalling the decks of a ship – clad the interiors.
The transparency of the façade, with its almost invisible large sliding doors, completes the perfect readability of this building.
While the hotel is articulated to harmoniously match the profile of the promontory, pushing it towards the horizon, the yacht-club pavilion rests between the hanging gardens and pools of water with its simple geometric shape, enriched by its envelope of large built-in vertical transparent panels, alternating with stone and teak.
The architectural language of the residences is defined by the overlapping wooden terraces, which contain the continuous ribbon of the façade.
This sequence of overlapping but not aligned planes creates a harmonic and complex disorder, communicating a truly elegant but not formal environment, exclusive but open to spectacular views of the surroundings.
The project aims to integrate with the shapes and intentions present in the island, and become a part of it: the use of a limestone reminiscent of the golden sand of the desert, but also sculpted architecture of southern Italy, engenders continuity with natural materials and the man-made of which the island is composed.
The boundary walls, podiums, and system's most solid parts are clad in golden limestone; while lava stone and basalt paving create a refined graphic contrast for the public spaces, which are treated as an "inner" urban environment.
The project assembles iconic features of great communicative power, expressing the state-of-the-art Bulgari luxury while simultaneously incorporating the uniqueness of each destination.
Adopting a pale colour palette and a predominance of Italian marble, the firm capitalized on the natural light in Dubai. At the same time, the architects provided shade from the Dubai sun using *brise soleils* or matte white lacquered steel parapets – a nod to the traditional Arabic approach to shading from the sun, which became an iconic part of the resort's architectural design.

Kindred spirits in their approach to luxury living, Antonio Citterio, Patricia Viel, and Bulgari wished to create a whole new hotel concept geared towards exceptional guest comfort, convenience, and services with undoubted Italian flair. Building this concept from scratch, their contemporary design recreates true comfort in the midst of luxury across the hotels and resorts. The designer furniture in every room and public areas include the finest Italian brands, such as Maxalto, Flos, Flexform, B&B Italia, created from the most exquisite materials.
Modern and minimalistic, the Bulgari Resort Dubai dovetails superior quality materials with tasteful Bulgari touches. Embodying bold contrasts, clean, regal lines, and the ubiquity of spaciousness, the property maintains an impeccable elegance, creating a continuity that permeates every detail.

[1] The development of manmade islands, waterfronts, and resorts across the region was conceived to transform the coastline in preparation for a post-oil economy and thus increase tourism. Examples of this trend are the well-known Palm Jumeirah, Palm Jebel Ali and The World (a set of islands that resemble a world map). These projects are visible from outer space and as yet only partially realized. It is worth mentioning that the luxury Burji Al Arab hotel is also built on an artificial island: see Y. Elsheshtawy, *Dubai: Behind an Urban Spectacle* (Routledge, 2009), pp. 142–45.

AXIOM Telecom Headquarter

Architecture and Interior Design: MMA Projects

Project Management Office: Dynamic Design Consultants

Client: Axiom Telecom LLC

Location: Dubai Silicon Oasis, Dubai, UAE

Completed in: 2018

Area: 34,000 sq.m

Top: Detail of the interconnection of building volumes made in concrete, corten steel, and glass.

View of the north-east corner of the building and the parking zone. The entrance from this side allows access to the building's common areas (conference rooms, restaurant and bar, gym, and pool).

Left: Axiom Telecom HQ Interiors, 2018. Stairs and walkways connect the building's multifunctional areas, where public and private spaces intertwine harmoniously.

Above: The internal green areas, the natural light coming from the broad windows, and the varied surfaces of wood and stone create a continuum between outside and inside.

The building is the headquarter of Axiom Telecom, the leading telecommunication company in the UAE.
Located in a high-density technological area as Dubai Silicon Oasis, the new landmark is conceived as a journey through a visionary city suspended between industry and nature, in a constant balance between public and private space.
The project designed by the Italian studio MMA Projects is the result of the work carried out on four fundamental assumptions and their relationships: Icon and Green Building, City, Garden, and Technology. In addition to the guidelines recommended by the client, four further features were added: Impact, Presence, Recognizability, and Synesthesia. The design process pivots entirely on these concepts, giving life to a massive building that is at the same time suspended and balanced. Concrete, black glass, and corten steel are the three essential materials used to shape the sculptural volume of the building whose forms evoke an ancient stone.
The architectural structure rises around a central garden: a green heart that extends equally in indoor and outdoor spaces.
The external concrete envelope presents various gaps through which people can enter, and which allow natural light to filter inside. It creates a suggestive atmosphere internally and intriguing perspectives where, in equal measure, both public and private multifunctional areas intertwine harmoniously.
A corten steel roof visually connects the various fragments. It is the sum of many-faceted elements that wrap and connect the structure as a whole. At the same time, large black glass windows merge with the different elements and further connect everything as dark markings between the "shield split".
Internally, the general plan of the Headquarters is divided into three main blocks with separate functions: the main aggregation area comprising restaurant, lounge bar, gym, spa, and conference room; a central area dedicated to the operational and managerial activity; and lastly, the R&D and logistics operations area, which perfectly integrate with the rest of the building. These three zones are joined via internal walkways forming lanes that penetrate the different buildings. In particular, the two raised floors are linked to each other through an intersection of stairs and metal bridges, while part of the top storey is designed as an ample open space that becomes a hanging garden suspended over the central greenspace.
The gardens offer a mixture of low and tall trees, stone and wood surfaces, water mirrors, and lighting, a fluid ensemble that ensures continuity between outside and inside, providing a unique sense of place.
The interior is characterized by its seamless balance between operational functions and relational spaces, a new experience of the office environment, where collaboration between people is pivotal to the project as a whole.
The Axiom Telecom Headquarter is a striking example of simple complexity, and offers a new reference standard for office premises. The project won the Plan Award 2015 in the Office & Business category of future projects. It has also been voted among the best projects in 2019 on the international online platform Architizer.

The Constellation (The Founder's Memorial)

Company: Maeg Costruzioni

Design: Ralph Helmick

Client: Private Office of Sheikh Mohammed bin Zayed Al Nahyan / MUSANADA

Contractor: Al Fara'a Engineering General Contracting

Location: Al Ras Al Akhdar, Abu Dhabi, UAE

Period of execution: 2017–2018

The Constellation is a monumental public artwork that forms the centrepiece of the Founder's Memorial Park, a permanent national tribute to commemorate the life, legacy, and values of the UAE's founding father.

The project was kept secret until its unveiling in February 2018, on the occasion of the commencement of the Year of Zayed, to mark the 100th anniversary since the birth of Sheikh Zayed.

Designed by the American sculptor and public artist Ralph Helmick b. 1952, Pittsburgh, USA), the Constellation comprises a dynamic three-dimensional silhouette of the face of Sheik Zayed. The sculpture, housed within a prismatic 30-metre-high custom-built pavilion at the heart of the park, has an overall weight of 250 tons. The structure consists of 1,327 geometric elements attached to 1,110 Inox steel cables. These suspended shapes constitute varying sizes of the five convex polyhedrons known as Platonic solids, "sacred geometries" renowned for their mathematical beauty and symmetry. Illuminating the sculpture in the late evening and during the night are 753 custom-made downlights and 1,203 uplights.

The monument to the emir can be experienced from multiple points of view by walking around the memorial, which offers continual discovery of new facets. In fact, the artwork constantly evolves with the changing light of day, while in the evening it is lit by over 2,000 light sources hidden in the roof and deck of the pavilion, creating a very suggestive atmosphere. The hanging solids shine like stars in the night sky, evoking a celestial display similar to a constellation.

Drawing on its wide expertise, Maeg Costruzioni designed, produced, and installed all the steel structures present in the project. The success of this prestigious scheme relied on the development of a unique and practical engineering solution aimed to overcome the challenges it presented, and achieved a perfect design solution.

In 2019 the Constellation won the prestigious CODA award (Collaboration of Design + Art, celebrating the projects that most successfully integrate commissioned art into interior, architectural, or public spaces) for international Institutional Artwork.[1]

[1] From the artist website https: //helmicksculpture.com/work/the-constellation.

[3] "The Founder's Memorial in Abu Dhabi wins global art and design award" (30 September 2019), *The National*: https://www.thenationalnews.com/arts-culture/the-founder-s-memorial-in-abu-dhabi-wins-global-art-and-design-award-1.916999 (accessed 21 June 2021).

The Constellation monument set amidst a lush green garden, 2018.

Ladies Club

Architecture and Interior Design: Urbanism Planning Architecture – UPA Consultancy & UPA Italia

Client: Abu Dhabi Sports Council

Location: Abu Dhabi, UAE

Period of execution: 2008–2018, currently under expansion

Area: 180,000 sq.m, 21,000 sq.m (BuA)

Built near the crystal sea of the Persian Gulf, the Club is an exclusive oasis of wellbeing and relaxation dedicated exclusively to women. It is a luxury venue where women can experience in complete privacy all the pleasures of fitness and body-care.
The projects date back to 2008.
The architecture firm UPA, was in charge of the entire masterplan covering an immense area of 180,000 sq.m, including the design of the various internal and external spaces.
Designed by the architects Paolo Lettieri and Aswan Zubaidi, the compound comprises the Main Club House Building (approximately 21,000 sq.m), which includes several facilities: a restaurant, a cafeteria, a lounge area, a VIP section, a fitness area, and a semi-Olympic indoor swimming pool with a relaxation zone offering whirlpools, shops and boutiques, and the music school.
The modern and organic architecture of the Club recalls floral forms in plan: the client's request was to have a unique, highly iconic building without rigid shapes.
The resulting sinuous forms generate fluid and unusual spaces that make this architecture strongly characterized and unique. The floral section embraces a semi-covered central enclosure called the Festival Space, which houses the outdoor swimming pool and solarium area, overlooking a private park and beach. In front of the beach, a lagoon separated from the open sea has been created, with a series of strips of land and breakwaters. In this way, women are free to swim and sunbathe far from any prying eyes and curious boats.
The façade of the building is entirely clad with stone, the main structure is

The outdoor swimming-pool. The view highlights the building's curvilinear profile, which define the open space area.

in reinforced concrete, while the two coverings of the entrance and the festival space are in metal lattices. The floors throughout are laid with prestigious marble. Precious elements also characterize the interiors. Of particular interest is the indoor swimming pool: its surfaces are entirely faced with Gold Onyx Maximum ceramic slabs created by the Italian firm Fiandre Architectural Surfaces, well known for their high-quality products and advanced solutions.
The marble-effect ceramic material is enriched by a glossy finish obtained by post-production treatment with rough diamond heads, giving a brilliant effect and creating a sophisticated environment. LED strip-lighting is embedded directly into the slabs in a staggered pattern, generating a visual play of reflections with the polished onyx ceramics and the pool's water surface.
The Club House was inaugurated in June 2018 and the great success of the structure led UPA to design an extension. In particular, one of the structure's "petals" was redesigned to accommodate an extension to the fitness room (bringing it to over 1,800 sq.m) and a new gym and aerobics rooms, covering a total of 2,500 extra square metres. This part is currently under construction at the time of writing, and expected to be ready by 2024.
The complex also provides an area dedicated to outdoor sports, including a regular soccer field with stands and changing rooms (500 sq.m), and surrounded by an athletics track, tennis courts, and a shed for small boats and water-sports equipment.
The opening of the first Ladies Club with sports facilities, its expansion, and the new Sport Academy, coincide with an awareness of the importance of sport and movement in the Emirate society in recent years. According to the Sport Council, this innovative structure for a Middle Eastern country will help promote sports activities for the female world.

Above: Ladies Club exterior, 2021. Within the facility compound, it is under construction on the left side of the building, the Ladies Sports Academy, whose architecture and interior design has been appointed to UPA.

Below: View of the interior swimming-pool. The undulating ceiling with the shiny ceramic slabs and the embedded strip-lights ensure a solid, harmonic visual impact.

Preatoni Tower

Company: Preatoni Real Estate Development LLC

Project Management and Engineering: LC&Partners

Location: Jumeirah Lake Towers, Dubai, UAE

Period of execution: 2015–2019

Completed in: 2018

Area: 65,500 sq.m

The Dubai Star Tower, later renamed Preatoni Tower, offers a fascinating chapter of architecture in the panorama of Dubai's construction history.
Located at the upmarket JLT cluster in Dubai, the construction was proposed in 2005 and then officially started in 2007. However, when it had reached 40% in the construction stage, its initial developer froze the project in light of the economic crisis that hit the region in 2009–10. The building frame remained incomplete until 2014, when the Italian developer Preatoni Group decided to rescue and resuscitate the entire project. Thanks to the support and cooperation of the local authorities, Dubai Land Department, and the investors, Preatoni took over and entrusted the project management to the Italian company LC&Partners. Holding the role of Client Representative and Construction Project Management Consultant, LC&Partners managed the reactivation of the construction site in 2016, ensuring the tower's completion. Its team successfully solved the legacy of technical, logistical, administrative, and bureaucratic issues arising from its troubled history. Indeed, during the almost ten-year duration of the construction site and the long intermediate phase in which work was suspended, many were the changes in contracting companies, legislation, and construction standards that took place.
Officially completed in 2018, the Preatoni Tower is among Dubai's 90 tallest high-rise buildings, with a height of 196 metres.[1] The 45-storey mixed-use tower "boasts 554 units covering a total of 600,000 sq.ft of prime residential and commercial space".[2]

[1] Data taken from The Skyscraper Center Database maintained by the Council of Tall Buildings and Urban Habitat (CTBUH): http://skyscrapercenter.info/building/preatoni-tower/8950 and is accurate as of September 2021.
[2] "Stalled 'Dubai Star' Tower completed after 4 years from rescue" (20 January 2019), *Gulf Insider*: https://www.gulf-insider.com/stalled-dubai-star-tower-completed-4-years-rescue/ (accessed 26 September 2021).

View of The Preatoni Tower, 2018. The skyscraper rises in the Jumeirah Lake Towers (JLT), an urban development constructed along three artificial lakes in Dubai.

PREATONI
TOWER JLT

The Scroll Monument

Company: RIMOND AEC
Design and Engineering: Gerry Judah (artist) with Diales (engineer)
Client: Sharjah Investment and Development Authority, Shurooq
Location: Sharjah, UAE
Period of execution: 2018–2019

The Scroll is a monumental sculpture that stands in front of the House of Wisdom, an iconic library and cultural centre designed by the international architects Foster + Partners.
Inspired by the institution of the same name dating from the Abbasid Caliphate in Baghdad,[1] the library is a knowledge hub where groups of all ages and nationalities can seek enrichment and social engagement. The centre is a model for how libraries in the future will blend traditional and digital knowledge sources and interactive learning.
Commanding the landscape before the House of Wisdom unfurls the Scroll Monument. Designed by the British artist Gerry Judah (b. 1951, Kolkata, India) and engineered by Diales, the construction of the artwork was completed and delivered by RIMOND.
The shape is a contemporary interpretation of the ancient Arabic scrolls, a single, spiralling sculpture that loops towards the sky, in contrast with the minimalist lines of the library building opposite. It is conceived as an artistic expression of cultural tolerance and exchange. Rising some 36 metres and comprising 72 tons of steel with 240 tons of concrete foundations, the sculpture's curved shell is composed of plates of laser-cut rolled steel, welded together and painted with multiple layers to protect the steel from erosion.
The sculpture was unveiled in April to celebrate Sharjah's designation as the UNESCO World Book Capital 2019.

[1] The House of Wisdom in Baghdad was founded in 830 CE by Caliph Harun Al-Rashid of the Abbasid Caliphate (r. 786–809 CE) during the so-called Islamic Golden Age. It was a library that preserved manuscripts and rare books in various languages about the arts and the sciences. Al-Rashid's son, Al-Ma'mun (r. 813–833) enlarged the original collection and turned it into an academy of knowledge named Bayt al-Hikma (the House of Wisdom). It is important to underline that no tangible trace remains of it.
J. Al Khalili, *The House of wisdom: how Arabic science saved ancient knowledge and gave us the Renaissance* (New York: Penguin Press, 2011), pp. 89–100.

The Scroll's monumental spiralling figure at night rises up from a green hill across from the House of Knowledge, 2019.

Akoya Nursery School

Architecture Design: Studio Costa Architecture

Client: Hisham Mansour

Location: Dubai, UAE

Period of execution: 2016–2019

Area: 2,084 sq.m

The Akoya Nursery school is located in a new district in Dubai called Akoya Oxygen.
Designed by the Italian consultants Studio Costa Architecture, the project's vision is based on a pedagogic ethos of inclusivity, learning in synergy with nature, and ecological responsibility. This concept is aligned with studio's hallmark "New Humanism" approach that puts "the human factor before all others, based on understanding and anticipating the future expectations of the people who will inhabit the cities of tomorrow".[1]

The project comprises the design and construction of a modern high-quality nursery for children from infant to pre-school ages.
It is conceived as a suspended architecture above a sunken playground, an open-air court in which the interior and exterior form a visual continuity, an effect given by the glazed curtain wall of the internal façade. As in a pavilion with continual connections with the landscape, it encourages indoor and outdoor activities.
All spaces of the various services enclosed in colourful volumes are situated around the central court,

Exterior of the school, 2019.

Opposite: View of the internal open playground.

where a tree – symbolizing knowledge and growth – rises in the middle.
A large canopy-roof and a shade structure protect the court from the direct sunshine, generating an autonomous micro-climate.
As in a home, children grow in a protected environment in which every detail is designed and thought for them: natural materials and modular furniture elements, easy to move, were chosen to arrange the classroom with the flexibility to accommodate changing daily educational activities.
The integrated signage system inspired iconographically by the natural and animal world generates a playful nursery environment and creates an atmosphere where imagination and creativity are the primary means of education.
The project has been awarded as Best Education Project of the Year at Design Middle East Awards 2019.[2]

[1] https://www.studiocosta.ae/.
[2] R. Arora (31 October 2019), "Design Middle East Awards 2019: Complete list of winners!" *Design Middle East*. https://design-middleeast.com/design-middle-east-awards-2019-complete-list-of-winners/

United Arab Emirates Space Agency Building

Company: Cimolai, Rimond Middle East General Contracting LLC[1]

Architecture Design: Foster + Partners

Client: Abu Dhabi Future Energy company PJSC–Masdar

Location: Masdar City, Abu Dhabi, UAE

Period of execution: 2016–2019

As the main contractor for the construction of United Arab Emirates pavilion for Expo 2015 Milan, RIMOND conducted the building's design development and construction, combining their finest practices and technology with a lean construction approach.
Following the closure of Expo 2015 Milan, Cimolai Rimond Middle East General Contracting was appointed by Masdar[2] to dismantle and relocate the UAE pavilion to Abu Dhabi, and reassemble it as headquarters for the UAE Space Agency. The rebuilding in a prominent site next to the Masdar Institute in Masdar City was completed in the first quarter of 2019. Designed by international architects Foster + Partners, the pavilion's undulating walls stand 12 metres high. The impressive structure references the UAE's historic urban settlements, which were characterized by narrow self-shaded streets, and to the magnificent open sand dunes of the desert. To convey a distinctive sense of place, the design of the walls derives from 3D scans of dune surfaces taken in the desert to create an authentic texture.
A steel frame supports the glass-fibre reinforced concrete panels. The building includes office spaces with maximized daylight use from a skylight, along with a green oasis in the middle of the building.
The design follows the principles of LEED,[3] with a combination of passive and active techniques.

View of the entrance to the UAE Pavilion at Expo Milan 2015 by Foster + Partners, now home of the UAE Space Agency Headquarters in Abu Dhabi, Masdar City. After the exhibition, the pavilion was dismantled and relocated to the UAE capital.

Opposite top right: Walkways and steps through the narrow open street in the pavilion, Milan 2015. From the photo one can notice the varied textures and materials (concrete and glass) of the high walls.

Opposite bottom: Overhead view of the courtyard with its curved and sinuous reinforced concrete panels, whose undulating pattern evokes the desert sands, also in its colours, Milan 2015.

[1] The company Cimolai Rimond Middle East General Contracting LLC does not exist anymore. It was established in Abu Dhabi in 2016. Today the companies maintain their autonomy respectively as Cimolai S.p.A. and RIMOND Middle East General Contracting L.L.C.
[2] Masdar is a global leader in renewable energy and sustainable urban development. Established in 2006 and owned by the Abu Dhabi Government's Mubadala Investment Company, Masdar advances clean technologies and supports the UAE's transition towards a knowledge-based economy. The Company is in charge of the development of Masdar City, a sustainable urban development that relies entirely on renewable energies and high clean technology and whose master plan is designed by the London architecture firm Foster + Partners. For more information about the company visit the website: www.masdar.ae. Regarding the Masdar urban development www.masdarcity.ae.
[3] Leadership in Energy and Environmental Design (LEED) is a system used to rate green buildings, awarding certification to acknowledge sustainability achievement and leadership.

Villa Sogno

Architecture Design: Whitespace Architects

Client: Private

Location: Al Khawaneej, Dubai UAE

Period of execution: 2019

Area: 800 sq.m

Villa Sogno, 2021, is a minimalist expression of forms.

Top: The interior plays with vertical structure and glass transparency, while the exterior horizontally offsets the flooring and the water pools distributed around the villa.

Villa Sogno, pool deck at night. The water's surface and strategic lighting create an intriguing play of reflexions, creating a suspended atmosphere.

Below: View from the living area, an open space communicating with the outside through a wide window accentuating the effect of transparency while blurring the distinction between interior space and the courtyard.

Located in Al Khawaneej, a desert area on the western side of Dubai, Villa Sogno is designed by Whitespace Architects – an Italian international design practice with a base in Dubai (founded by Francesco Anzolin, Yasser Abuelnasr and Khalid Alansari) – to embrace its environment and blend into the surrounding golden dunes. The simple design carves into a clean rectangular mass, creating the indoor and outdoor living spaces and accentuating the clean, modern architectural lines.
The beige travertine stone is predominant in both interior rooms and exterior extensions with the addition of warm full-height wooden walls. The earthy colours, with the subtle landscaping and water feature, allow smooth incorporation with the surrounding desert. Thus, the villa complements its surrounding as if coming from within instead of standing out and interrupting the calm sandy shades.
The one-story villa features a family space consisting of living-room, dining-room, and open kitchen areas overlooking the main landscaped courtyard with its infinity pool that connects to the spa and gym area, offering a calming, meditative environment.

Dubai Digital Park

Company: Laminam

Client: Dubai Silicon Oasis Authority

Consultant: Design and Architecture Bureau (DAR)

Contractor: China State Construction Engineering Coorporation LLC

Location: Dubai Silicon Oasis, Dubai, UAE

Period of execution: 2017

Completed: 2020

Announced as Dubai's first smart city, Dubai Digital Park combines contemporary design, sustainability, and technology. Designed by DAR – Design and Architecture Bureau, it comprises 96,000 square metres divided into office and commercial space, and 46,000 square metres of residential property. The overall masterplan comprises two hill-like podiums separated by a metaphorical river of public space. To enhance the convenience of its approximately 2,000 employees and residents, the masterplan is equipped with high-performance technology that comprises both exterior and interior: digital signage, smart kiosks, robotic technology, and weather sensors accompanied by smart benches, parks, ticketing, as well as child ID and tagging. The technology extends further to the domestic experience, with smart home automation.
The large format and minimum thickness made Laminam's slabs the perfect choice to clad the façades of the buildings.

View of the building façade clad with Laminam's ceramic slabs.

Opposite: Detail of the Dubai Digital Park area, 2021. It is a mixed environment giving onto a plaza designed to integrate living and business spaces.

The numbers are impressive: 60,000 sq.m of ceramic slabs applied with wet fixing façade of Laminam 3+ proved to meet the performance standards stipulated in the project brief.
Premium Italian quality and aesthetics merge in both "Collection" and "I Naturali", the

two series chosen from the wide Laminam product range.
Elegant and well measured, the "Collection" series incorporates the concept of versatility par excellence, with its full-bodied colour, perfect for distinguishing the seamless continuity of spaces and volumes. Like all other Laminam ceramic slabs, the "Collection" series is built to stand the test of time; no colour fading from exposure to sunlight, nor surface deterioration due to wear and tear.
The "I Naturali" series establishes a new canon of elegance and solemnity transposed to large ceramic slabs, immune to the passing of time, while defining a new aesthetic paradigm. Resistant to impact, stains, and scratches, these surfaces retain their specifications even when exposed to heat, frost, and UV rays, with average water absorption of 0.1%.

Etihad Arena

Company: ItalMesh

Architecture Design: HOK
with the support of Pascall + Watson

Client: MIRAL

Main Contractor: BAM International

Location: Yas Island, Abu Dhabi, UAE

Period of execution: 2019–2021

Area: 25,000 sq.m

The Etihad Arena is the largest and most state-of-the-art indoor entertainment venue in the Middle East. Located on the lively waterfront of Yas Bay on Yas Island, it is a flexible venue devised to adapt to a wide range of events. Designed by HOK with the support of Pascall + Watson, the arena was completed in 2021.
The iconic design is inspired by the intertwined meshes of the baskets used by the Bedouin tribes, translated into a modern structure contextualizing the building with the country's history. ItalMesh, an Italian company specialized in implementing architectural projects using expanded metal mesh and perforated panels, participated in the design, engineering, and construction of all the modules used for the cladding of the arena's façades. The technicians conducted the study for over a year to find the ideal solution for installing over 28,000 expanded mesh panels. The ItalMesh team followed every phase of the engineering and production processes, verifying the aesthetic and functional aspects, with engineers and architects in charge of the work. Precisely for this reason, ItalMesh selected high-quality raw materials and finishes that guaranteed long-lasting performance. The Etihad Arena is a modern architectural structure offering 100% sustainability, thanks to its advanced design solutions.
The design of the building's gold membrane is environmentally responsive, as it allows control of climate resistance reducing the solar heat.

View of the Etihad Arena, along the coast of Yas Bay waterfront, district of Yas Island, 2021. The gold shell made of metal mesh panels by ItalMesh combines aesthetics, functionality, and resistance.

Al Raha Lofts

Architecture Design: M+N Architecture (for plot C5), iBridge Engineering – Cotefa. ingegneri&architetti (for plot C20)

Client: Reportage Real Estate

Main Contractor: A&M International

Location: Al Raha Beach, Abu Dhabi, UAE

Period of execution: 2017–2022

Area: for plot C5 – 14,554 sq.m (GFA), 30,230 sq.m (BuA), for plot C20 – 9,015 sq.m (GFA), 20,000 sq.m(BuA)

The Al Raha Lofts is a residential building forming part of Al Raha Beach waterfront development in the east part of Abu Dhabi. The idea behind the development was to create a unique complex comprising duplex apartments with internal stairs connecting the two levels. From this detail, the development took the name of "Al Raha Lofts" to recall the loft apartment typology of New York and Europe.

The residential complex comprises two separate buildings connected at the podium level with communal facilities (sport courts and kids play areas).

Even though both buildings share similarities in their architecture, they have been designed by two different Italian architecture studios: M+N Architecture, and iBridge Engineering in collaboration with Cotefa.ingegneri&architetti.

M+N Architecture was tasked with the design of the larger of the two buildings, which spreads over nine levels and includes 164 residential units of various types, 14 retail units, two levels of underground parking, a shared swimming pool, a gym, a central laundry, and a reception area with a security chamber.

The building faces the main road (Al Raha Boulevard) and the open sea (visible in between the nearby buildings), while the other side overlooks the artificial canal and promenade. To maximize the exposure of the apartments to the natural light providing each unit with a private balcony, the building has an E-shape with three wings protruding towards the canal, with tiered setbacks that create a softer visual impact.

The elevation facing the main road is more regular in shape and visually interacts with the constructions nearby, the city roads, and walkways.

Due to the difference in level between the main road and the canal's promenade, the podium contains the two-level of parking on one side, while some duplex units have direct access to the promenade. On top of the podium are located the swimming pool and other communal areas.

Close up of the Al Raha Lofts façade design by M+N Architecture.

800 ALDAR
ALDAR.COM

The façades are clad with panels in different shades of the same hue, and include vertical linear shading structures connecting the slabs of the balconies, creating more dynamic and irregular frontage to soften the overall masses.
The complex designed fully in-house by iBridge Engineering – Cotefa.ingegneri&architetti Group includes 110 residential units. Most of them are duplex apartments spread over six levels.
The design aimed to organize the levels to allow for the greatest number of apartments. The building layout offers an E-shape designed to provide the best views of the waterfront and landscape.
The plan and section configuration facilitate the movement of air along the canal thanks to the sloping section. The gaps in the façade form air channels for the pool deck, and the central area of the apartment complex.
The interior design is modern, with basic volumes that amplify the space surrounded by ample windows and gentle colours.
The materials used are warm and natural, such as wood, stone, and marble.
Typical of a loft, the internal staircase is visible from the outside, and acts both as a connecting architectural element and as an aesthetic feature.
The façade is covered by shading devices that follow the sloping profile of the building and enhance the living quality of the inhabitants.
The entire complex of two buildings complies with the Pearl 1 rating of Estidama, the Abu Dhabi standard for sustainable construction. It is designed according to the most advanced industry standards for insulation and glazed façades, including thermal modelling to assess the building's responsiveness to the extreme conditions of Abu Dhabi's climate.
At the time of publication, the buildings are in their final stage of construction. The apartments are all sold out, confirming the project's success in terms of design and positive feedback from the local market.

Above: View of Al Raha Lofts along the street designed by iBridge Engineering and Cotefa ingegneri&architetti. While the one at the end, on the right, is by M+N Architecture. The two buildings are very close to each other and, at first glance, seem similar in design.

Right: View of the protruding building façades with the open vista on the artificial navigable canal and promenade.

Oasis Residences

Architecture Design: iBridge Engineering – Cotefa.ingegneri&architetti

Client: Reportage Real Estate – Elige Real Estate

Main Contractor: A&M International General Contracting – Dogma General Contracting

Location: Masdar City, Abu Dhabi, UAE

Period of execution: 2017–2022

Area: Oasis 1: 35,683 sq.m (GFA), 71,400 sq.m (BuA) - Oasis 2: 18,500 sq.m (GFA), 40,300 sq.m (BuA)

The Oasis Residences project is a residential complex of two buildings located in the sustainable urban development of Masdar City. Designed by the Italian Group iBridge Engineering – Cotefa. ingegneri&architetti, the two buildings are similar in design but differ in size. Oasis 1, occupying a plot of 8,371 sq.m, consists of 612 residential apartments spread over ten storeys, while Oasis 2 in a plot of 6,458 sq.m comprises 304 residential apartments located in a ten-storey tower. Both buildings are enriched with an exclusive pool deck with two swimming pools and courtyards with shaded areas and abundant greenery.

The aim of the architects was to develop a building that fulfilled the requirements exceeding expectations in terms of residential space while respecting the significance and "green print ideology" of Masdar City.

Considering the particular settlement area's climatic conditions, the design choices adopted a mix of traditional Arabic architectural elements for natural building ventilation, along with *mashrabiya* panels as cooling barriers. This conventional amalgam was injected with modern technology to maximize energy efficiency.

These ambitions aims were achieved by focusing on the architectural and technological elements, conceiving the building not merely as a multi-functional and versatile box with new energy technologies applied as an afterthought to resolve internal comfort issues, but by applying a design approach that prioritizes formal and technological solution integration in compliance with the Masdar masterplan recommendations.

The superb result is a U-shaped complex, open to the green belt area, and at the same time offering precision circulation control adapted to sunlight throughout the year, in order to maximize the shade needed during the summer, and exploit the more gentle light during the winter. A balanced compromise between a compact shape that reduces dispersions and creates shaded areas in the courtyard and an open volume that funnels the natural light.

To expand the passive energy performance of the building, a carefully chosen variety of plants were provided, so as to contribute both high- and low-pressure areas in the building's neighbourhood. These planned green areas convey a natural ambient flows in correspondence with the building's windows, enhancing the overlooking façades and supporting the building's natural ventilation.

Particular attention has also been paid to the deployment of diverse materials in order to maximize thermal comfort for the external settings and the internal ventilation of habitable units.

Solar screens made of perforated and bent aluminium sheets with a triangle shape section will be anchored to the building's façades, elements that guarantee a high-performance shield against the glaring sun. Thanks to the high heat dissipation capacity of wide surfaces in aluminium, the solar screens greatly improve air circulation around the building. Meanwhile, insulated panels guarantee thermal buffers on the balconies of reinforced concrete. The railings are made of transparent glass to ensure proper internal illumination, whether sunlight or reflection.

Currently, under construction, Oasis 1 is scheduled to be finished in Q2 2022, while the Oasis 2 building is planned for completion in Q4 2022.

The development complex prides itself on being awarded a 3 Pearl building rating for surpassing the Estidama Energy and Sustainability regulations.

Above: Construction site of the Oasis Residences, 2021.

Oasis Residences in Masdar city, 2021. The whole architecture is environmentally responsive.

Umm Lafina Link Road

Company: Webuild

Client: Department of Transport Abu Dhabi (DoT)

Contractor: Webuild 60% – Tristar Joint Venture Sit JV

Location: Abu Dhabi, UAE

Period of execution: 2018–ongoing (nearing completion)

Length: 4 km (of 10.5 km)

Umm Lafina Link Road is a high profile project constructed with cutting-edge bridging technologies, while its engineering and architectural features can be considered a contemporary work of art.
The bridge provides access to Umn Lafina which is currently a virgin island that will be developed with high-end residential complexes. One of the major challenges is that the road had to be constructed above the national mangrove park, a protected area that is known as the "lungs" of Abu Dhabi. This area is of great landscape value and extreme environmental sensitivity. Therefore, in line with the sustainability objectives stipulated by the Abu Dhabi Government, the project integrates all the necessary measures to ensure its functional and landscape integration in a harmonious way with the context, as well as its implementation in full

compliance with ecological parameters and environmental sustainability.
The project is part of the "Abu Dhabi 2030" development plan as the main element of the MIP Road Network, the new road system connecting the Capital District and the Central Business District, currently under development on Al Reem Island.
The contract includes the design and subsequent construction of the first section of the road link between Sheikh Zayed bin Sultan Street – the main access highway to Abu Dhabi – and the island of Al Reem, passing through the island of Umm Lafina. The route includes a motorway junction, two bridges and an arched viaduct, approximately 4 km length.

Umm Lafina nature reserve, Abu Dhabi, 2018.
As part of the Abu Dhabi 2030 Development Plan, the project aims to ensure the improvement of infrastructure to reduce traffic congestion and support economic growth in Abu Dhabi Emirate. The road construction passing over the mangrove forest seeks to preserve the natural environment, since the mangrove supports a unique ecosystem. Webuild will relocate and plant double the number of mangroves expected to be lost during the construction, in accordance with its sustainability principles.

Industrial Landscape

Borouge Complex

Company: Maire Tecnimont

Client: Abu Dhabi National Oil Company (ADNOC)

Location: Ruwais, Abu Dhabi, UAE

Date of Execution: 1999–2010

Maire Tecnimont started its significant involvement with Abu Dhabi National Oil Company (ADNOC) in 1999 with the construction of Borouge's first petrochemical complex in Ruwais, known as "Borouge 1". Meaning "tower" in Arabic, Borouge is a joint venture between ADNOC and Austria-based company Borealis. The complex transforms crude oil derivatives into various types of plastics of the kind used today in many advanced industrial applications.
In the wake of this successful delivery, Maire Tecnimont was also awarded the contracts to carry out the Engineering-Procurement-Construction (EPC) works of the two major plant expansions: "Borouge 2" in 2007 and "Borouge 3" in 2010, for a total value of more than US$ 4bn, and an overall production of more than 5 million tons of polymers per year. Borouge is one of the world's largest petrochemical complexes.

View of the Borouge 3 Polyolefins Complex in Ruwais, 2014.

Emirates Steel Complex

Company: Danieli & C. Officine Meccaniche

Client: Emirates Steel

Location: Mussafah, Abu Dhabi, UAE

Period of execution: 2006–2011

Area: 1.5 sq.km

Owned by SENAAT holding, in 2006 and 2008 Emirates Steel launched two phases of expansion of its steel plant as part of the ongoing commitment to support the growth of the non-oil industry sectors, in line with the Government's plan for the UAE's economic diversification. With the completion of the expansion plan, the plant was transformed from a basic processor of imported steel billets into the first and only "full-fledged integrated steel manufacturing facility in the UAE".[1]
Based in the Mussafah industrial area of Abu Dhabi, the expansion comprises a total area of 1.5 sq.km adjacent to the existing one.
Italian plantmaker Danieli was awarded the facility's turnkey supply for both phases, involving engineering, manufacturing, procurement and construction. Commissioning started in 2008. Phase 1, inaugurated in June 2009, served to build up an integrated steel plant consisting of a direct reduction plant utilizing Energiron technology and an associated steel meltshop.
The completion of Phase 2, in March 2011 (Phase 2A) and December 2011 (Phase 2B) respectively, doubled Emirates Steel's steelmaking capacity with a further expansion of the plant, designed by Danieli, and saw the construction of a heavy-section rolling mill – the first of its kind – with a production capacity of 1 million tons per year.

Night view of the Direct Reduction Plant at Emirates Steel, 2012.

Opposite: Steel Mill, Direct Reduction Iron Plant, 2011.

With the completion of the second phase, Emirates Steel started the production of new products, such as large steel beams and columns, sheet piles, channels, and angles, all at international standards. In 2017 Emirates Steel achieved an annual production record of more than 2 million tons of direct reduced iron in a single DRI module.[2]

[1] www. emiratessteel.com (accessed October 2021).
[2] https://www.danieli.com/en/news-media/news-events/emirates-steel-sets-new-record-dri-production_37_238.htm (accessed October 2021).

Jebel Ali Power and Desalination Plant

Company: Fisia Italimpianti (Webuild Group), Italengineering Middle East / Studio Geotecnico Nesti (Dubai Branch)

Client: Dubai Electricity and Water Authority (DEWA)

Contractor: Fisia Italimpianti (Webuild Group) and Doosan Heavy Industries & Construction

Location: Jebel Ali, Dubai, UAE

Period of execution: 2001–2012

Jebel Ali Power and Desalination Plant is the biggest plant to produce electricity and desalinated water in Dubai, with a production capacity of 2,400 megawatts.

It is situated along the shore of the Arabian Gulf in the proximity of the so-called Jebel Ali free zone in Dubai (UAE). The plant is part of the project developed by the Dubai Electricity and Water Authority (DEWA) to respond to the increasing demand for power and water in Dubai and support Dubai's comprehensive and sustainable development.[1]

The complex comprises two main plants, accommodating six stations in total (D, E, G, K, L, M). It was developed in several phases up to the final stage M that was commissioned in 2012. Jebel Ali M was the largest plant in the UAE when it was completed.[2]

Fisia Italimpianti, in a joint venture with Doosan Heavy Industries, was appointed as general contractor of the Jebel Ali Desalination Plant for G up to M stations. To the development of the complex, the Italian group Italengineering

Middle East–Studio Geotecnico Nesti was involved.
With their specialized roles as consultants in geotechnical, soil, and rock mechanics and foundation services, Italengineering Middle East–Studio Geotecnico Nesti provided engineering support and supervision during the construction phases.
The main issue encountered was soil characterization, the foundation design for the main structures, and earthworks.

A complex dewatering system was studied and designed for deep excavations under the groundwater table near the ground surface in equilibrium with the sea level. And marine work for the intake and outlet of the structures was carried out.
When station M, the final stage of the plant opened in 2013, it was the largest plant in the UAE with an "installed capacity of 2,060 megawatts and 140 million imperial gallons of water per day (MIGD)."[3] Each of the eight units has a production of 17.5 MIGD. The plant uses the Multi-Stage Flash process, which provides the flow of water necessary to the plant through big pipes that carry huge amounts of seawater from the Gulf, then pumped to a higher pressure and heated to near boiling through multiple stages.
In 2014, the plant was awarded "Desalination Plant of the Year" … "representing the industry's most impressive technical or ecologically sustainable achievement."[4]

[1] https://www.dewa.gov.ae/en/about-us/media-publications/latest-news/2021/07/jebel-ali-power-and-desalination-complex (accessed 15 October 2021).
[2] "Jebel Ali M Project" (25 February 2015), *Power Technology*: https://www.power-technology.com/projects/jebel-ali-m-station/ (accessed 15 October 2021).
[3] Ibid.
[4] https://globalwaterawards.com/2014-winners/ (accessed 26 November 2021).

Opposite: Detail of Jebel Ali Desalination Plant, 2017.

View of the Jebel Ali M Desalination Plant, 2017.

GASCO IGD Habshan 5

Company: Maire Tecnimont

Client: Abu Dhabi Gas Industries (GASCO)

Location: Abu Dhabi, UAE

Date of execution: 2009–2013

One of the largest gas treatment plants globally, Habshan 5 was developed to accommodate additional offshore gas production, along with associated gases that will become available as a result of the expansion of ADCO's[1] onshore oil production.
In a joint venture with JGC, in 2009 Maire Tecnimont was awarded by Abu Dhabi Gas Industries Ltd. (GASCO, part of the ADNOC Group) to carry out the EPC Works of IGD Habshan 5, for a value of US$ 4.7 bn. The project involved more than thirty thousand workers on site.
It was completed well ahead of schedule in 2013, with the world record of 100 million safe man-hours worked without any LTIs (lost time injuries, the primary on-site safety index), marking an unprecedented achievement in the industry. In 2013 Habshan 5 Project

was recognized as the "Best Gas & Oil Project" by the Abu Dhabi International Petroleum Conference (ADIPEC, the chief oil & gas event in the MENA area); in 2014 it was "Gold Winner" as project excellence in mega-sized projects by the International Project Management Association (IPMA). The production capacity of the plant is 2,150 MMSCFD of gas and 5,200 tons of sulphur/day.

[1] It is the Abu Dhabi Company for Onshore Oil Operations. In 2017 ADCO was renamed ADNOC Onshore following the Abu Dhabi National Oil Company's decision to unify the brand identity of its many operating units. "Adnoc launches a unified brand identity across its group of companies" (15 October 2017), *The Gulf News*: https://gulfnews.com/business/energy/adnoc-launches-a-unified-brand-identity-across-its-group-of-companies-1.2106361 (accessed 28 October 2021).

View on the Habshan 5 Gas Plant, considered one of the largest gas treatment plants worldwide, 2013.

Shah Gas Development Project Process Plant, Sulphur Recovery Unit and Product Pipelines

Company: Saipem

Client: ADNOC Sour Gas

Location: Shah, Abu Dhabi, UAE

Period of execution: 2010–2015; expansion in 2021

In 2010 Abu Dhabi Gas Development Company Limited awarded Saipem three EPC contracts as part of the Shah Gas development programme. The scheme was designed to treat 1 billion cubic feet a day of sour gas from the Shah Field, before separating the sulphur from the natural gas and transporting gas, condensate, and NGL from the Shah Gas Plant to processing facilities at Habshan area and ASAB tie in point through a nearly 250 kilometres of pipeline, and then to Ruwais, located in the west part of the Abu Dhabi Emirate.

Projects, executed through 3 EPC LSTK contracts, have represented a remarkable contribution to the growth and development of the entire region.

Process Plant and Sulphur Recovery Unit

The first two contracts included the engineering, procurement, and construction of the gas processing plant and the sulphur recovery unit. The plant is located in the Shah Field, approximately 100 km south of the existing ADNOC Gas Processing Habshan facility. Previously, there were no existing processing facilities at the Shah Gas Plant location. The complex can be considered the largest among the gas treatment plants for its specialized features. The high sour content and associated sulphur production makes HSE a fundamental pre-requisite of the entire plant design. This is especially for the inlet and gas sweetening facilities. The plant has a considerable extension of a 6x3 km footprint and is located within 3 low-lying area roots

facilities. It has an associated assembly quantity of about 80,000 tons of steel structure, 40,000 tons of piping, and 73,000 tons of equipment, of which 28,000 tons of heavy lifting machinery requiring special transportation and erection gear, and 5,400 km of electrical and instrumentation cabling.
Morover the Shah Gas Plant and Sulphur Recovery Units are 2 EPC packages of the Shah Gas Development Program, entailing 8 total EPC packages for a total number of 6 interfacing EPC contractors.
The remote location in the desert with its logistic challenges and the environmental constraints deriving from Saipem's commitment to minimize the footprint of large-scale operations in the area increased the degree of complexity in the project's execution.

Particular care was given to all site activities to ensure complete awareness and protection related to hazards to all workers, Saipem team, and subcontractors. Such an approach is in line with the LiHS (Leaders in Health and Safety) corporate programme introduced since the inception in the Shah Gas Project execution, with the aim to ensure HSE culture cascades through all levels of the workforce, from top management down to the on-site labourers.

Shah Product Pipelines Project
The Shah Product Pipelines Project was developed in the so-called Empty Quarter desert. The project consisted of three pipelines built to transport the products (sales gas, condensate, and NGL) from the Shah Gas Plant to existing networks plus 400 km of FOC (fibre-optic cable).
The Temporary Construction Facilities were assembled with due care to the environmental conditions of the areas. Special attention was paid to waste management, fuel storage, and other hydrocarbons, along with dust control and car monitoring management. This was done to control the location of vehicles in case of emergency, also limiting the access of non-authorized off-road excursions.
A camp site with on-site clinic was strategically built in the barycentre of the pipelines corridor to facilitate the construction mobilization crew. The location was nevertheless hard to reach for material delivery, handling, and transportation, as well as for resources mobilization.
Precaution and a special storage, maintenance and preservation procedures were implemented to preserve the construction materials, equipment, and consumables against the extreme temperatures (> 50°C) experienced during the summer. Special care went into the heat-stress management for all labourers, with dedicated training programme and continuously monitored precautions.
Other challenges sustained during the execution include the interface with other stakeholders (authorities, municipality, third-party owners) for the execution of over 300 crossings of existing facilities and networks.

Left: View of the Shah Gas development plant, 2014.

Above: Close up of the gas sulphur pipelines and the camp site built in the center of the pipelines corridor, 2014.

GASCO Sulphur Handling Terminal 2

Company: Techint Engineering & Construction

Client: GASCO – Abu Dhabi Gas Industries

Location: Ruwais, Abu Dhabi, UAE
(now ADNOC Gas Processing)

Period of execution: 2011–2016

Techint Engineering & Construction provides engineering, procurement, construction, operation, and management services for complex and large-scale projects worldwide. In particular, Techint Engineering Center in Italy offers high added-value services with its consolidated experience in the areas such as oil and gas, refinery, petrochemical plants, liquefied natural gas, power, industrial plants, healthcare and infrastructure, energy transition as well as cleantech.
One of its collaborations in the UAE is the project Sulphur Handling Terminal 2 in Ruwais, Abu Dhabi. The project involves engineering, procurement, construction, and commissioning for the construction of a storage and handling plant for about 20,000 tons of granulated sulphur per day.
Commissioned by GASCO (now ADNOC Gas Processing), the project began in January 2011. The first sulphur was introduced in late 2014, and the plant was handed over to the client in early 2016.

View of Ruwais Sulphur Handling Terminal 2, Abu Dhabi.
The project involves the rail unloading, granule storage, ship loading of granulated sulphur.

Etihad Rail

Companies: Saipem and Tecnimont, Swissboring (Trevi Group)

Client: Etihad Rail Company PJSC

Location: Abu Dhabi, UAE

Period of execution: 34 months, from 1 November 2011

Total length: 264 km (of 1,200 km)

View of the construction site of the 264 km of railway connecting gas fields in Shah and Habshan to an export point in Ruwais.

Opposite: Etihad Rail's Stage One has been completed. It has been providing services for freight and will provide services for passengers, reducing traffic and greenhouse gases. It will also facilitate access to the Al Dhafrah Region.

The UAE National Railway Network is 1,200 km long and extends from the Saudi Arabian border to the Port of Fujairah. It will be a mixed-used network with Freight Services connecting the Major Ports, Quarries, and Industrial Zones and Passenger Services connecting the cities of the United Arab Emirates.
Set to transform the UAE's transport infrastructure, it will form a vital part of the planned GCC rail network.
Etihad Rail was established in 2009 under federal law No.2 with the mandate to "manage the development, construction, and operation of the UAE's national freight and passenger railway network." [1]
The network's route departs from Ghweifat at Saudi Arabian to arrive in Abu Dhabi, then continues to Dubai, the northern Emirates, and Fujairah.
Designed in conformance with the most advanced international standards, Etihad Rail's network will "act as a catalyst for the country's economic growth, and sustained social development". [2]
Once completed, the railway network will redefine transport logistics throughout the entire region, providing a modern, safe, efficient, and eco-sustainable transport.
The project is divided into two stages, each one corresponding to a specific operation zone in the UAE.
The contract to carry out the Stage One of the project was awarded in 2011 to a consortium formed by the Italy-based Saipem and Tecnimont

(subsidiary of Maire Tecnimont), and the Indian contractor Dodsal Engineering. The project included the design, procurement, construction, testing, and commissioning of the 264-km network line infrastructure linking Shah and Habshan to Ruwais.
The year 2012 saw the start of the bored and cast *in situ* piling works for the corridors conducted by Swissboring (Trevi Group).
Stage One serves both the Habshan and Shah sour gas fields, and specifically is utilized for the transport of granulated sulphur deriving from oil processing from these fields to Ruwais. Since the start of operations in 2016 until June 2022 "Etihad Rail has transported more than 43 million tonnes of granulated sulphur, for the Abu Dhabi National Oil Company (ADNOC)".[3]
Most of the challenges encountered by Saipem and Tecnimont during the development of the rail network were mainly related to operating in a desert environment, with extreme weather conditions and topographic features.
Characterized by an impressive number of existing crossings, the railway passed through more than 50 km of sensitive desert areas of dunes reaching 150 metres, with 93 million m^3 of earthworks moved in two years.
Despite these hurdles, they delivered successfully and on time the entire Stage One. The project has been an example of sustainability, achieving full compliance with the Pearl Rating System of the UAE Estidama programme. Stage One has been commercially active since 2016.
Construction of Stage Two began in early 2020 with different contractors, and is currently under construction. Running for 605 km, the network will extend from Ghuwaifat on the border with Saudi Arabia to Fujairah on the UAE's eastern coast.
The first package of Stage Two from Ruwais towards Ghuwaifat and the Saudi Arabia border is now complete, and connects the existing 264 km Shah Habshan–Ruwais Stage One with the border of Saudi Arabia. The remaining packages of Stage Two are currently in progress. By 2030, the network line is expected to serve about 36.5 million passengers annually.[4]

[1] J. Coleman-Pecha and S. Kiryushin (19 April 2021), "Railway Regulation and Projects in the United Arab Emirates": https://dwfgroup.com/en/news-and-insights/insights/2021/4/railway-regulation-and-projects-in-the-united-arab-emirates (accessed 18 October 2021).
[2] From https://www.etihadrail.ae/etihad-rail-about/.
[3] From https://www.etihadrail.ae/project-update/. Following an agreement signed in October 2011, ADNOC became a customer of Etihad Rail for the transport of granulated sulphur from Habshan and Shah to Al Ruwais in Abu Dhabi for export: https://www.railway-technology.com/projects/etihad-rail/ (accessed 20 October 2021).
[4] R. Reynolds (5 December 2021), "Dubai to Abu Dhabi by train: Etihad Rail to expand to run passenger services", *The National*: https://www.thenationalnews.com/uae/transport/2021/12/05/uae-leaders-review-progress-on-etihad-rail-expansion/ (accessed 7 December 2021).

Independent Water and Power Plant

Company: Ansaldo Energia

Client: Abu Dhabi Water and Electricity Authority (ADWEA)[1]

Location: Mirfa, Abu Dhabi, UAE

Period of execution: 2015–2018

The first power and desalination plants built between Dubai and Abu Dhabi date back to the mid-1990s; Ansaldo Energia built the centre of Middle Eastern business development in this strategic point of the Arabian Peninsula.
One of Ansaldo Energia's pillars in the UAE is represented by the 1,500 Mirfa Independent Water and Power Plant project (IWPP), a built-in consortium with a Korean manufacturer between 2015 and 2018. The plant consists of 10 rotating machines (3 gas turbines, 2 steam turbines, and 5 turbo generators and relative auxiliary system), produced in the Genoa factory.
The installation in the United Arab Emirates of turbines designed and built by Ansaldo Energia has allowed the development of several long-term maintenance

The construction site of a Power and Desalination Plant along the coast of Mirfa (200 km west of Abu Dhabi), completed in mid-1990 by Ansaldo Energia.

contracts, which enable Ansaldo Energia to increase the trust placed in their company by customers in the Gulf.
The acquisition of these service contracts has been helped not only by the growing number of Ansaldo Energia turbines, but also by the ability to provide all essential maintenance services locally.
In particular, Ansaldo Energia Gulf workshop, which opened in 2010 and is dedicated to repairing turbo-gas components, guarantees Ansaldo Energia customers the certainty and comfort of having a centre of excellence in the country. Ansaldo Energia Gulf has achieved a leadership position in its sector during its short existence, having already completed more than 3,500 sets of components produced by Ansaldo Energia and its competitors.
Among the several service contracts acquired, special mention goes to the Taweelah power plant. Thanks to a first two-year service contract (already extended), here Ansaldo Energia carries out all the maintenance of 6 ABB steam turbines with the relative generators, 2 General Electric Turbogas with generators, on a ten-year contract for overall maintenance, which includes field interventions, replacement parts, and repairs of 3 Siemens turbo-gas units, for a total value of over 65 million euros.

[1] Today called EWEC (Emirates Water and Electricity Company).

Independent Water and Power Plant, Mirfa, 2017. The plant produces 1,600 mV of power and 52.5 million gallons of desalinated water per day (about 200,00 cubic metres). It is one of the nine desalination plants in Abu Dhabi.

Tenaris Industrial complex

Company: Tenaris

Client: Abu Dhabi National Oil Company (ADNOC)

Location: Abu Dhabi, UAE

Period of execution: 2019–2022

Area: 200,000 sq.m

Tenaris is a leading global manufacturer and supplier of steel pipe products and related services for the world's energy industry and other industrial applications. It has been present in the Middle East for over thirty years, and in 2010, it moved its eastern hemisphere headquarters to the UAE.
In 2019, Tenaris announced the development of a 200,000 sq.m industrial complex in Abu Dhabi, which includes an upgraded service hub, an industrial facility, and a training centre to better serve ADNOC, its key customer in the country.

Tenaris threading facility construction site in Abu Dhabi.

The construction of the threading facility is expected to finish by the second half of 2023, contributing towards industrialization in the UAE, and creating around 200 jobs in the market.

EXPO 2020 DUBAI
Connecting Minds, Creating the Future

Renewables
at the centre
of our strategy

EXPO 2020 Dubai: Connecting Minds, Creating the Future

Lucia Pizzinato

Expo 2020 Dubai opened its doors on 1 October 2021. (Although the Exhibition was pushed back a full year due to the coronavirus, the event kept the original title of Expo 2020 Dubai). It is the first international exhibition held in the MENASA region (Middle East, North Africa, South Asia). With the participation of 192 nations, each with their dedicated pavilion, Expo 2020 Dubai was the most diverse in the event's history and reflected the importance of being united for a better future. This concept is innate in the ancient Arabic name of Dubai's city Al Wasl, meaning connection.

The event's name was therefore the expression of the Expo's motto: "Connecting Minds Creating the Future". It underlined the significance of fostering creativity, innovation, and collaboration between countries, cultures, and institutions. It also inspired visitors to formulate new ways to develop shared solutions for the future.

Al Wasl is also the name of the site's main plaza, the focal point from which fan out the three petals highlighting the individual districts of the Expo's triad of sub-themes – Mobility, Opportunity, Sustainability.

These three themes were conceived and developed in the Expo masterplan of 155 hectares situated halfway between Abu Dhabi and Dubai. Each participating pavilion explored these themes, each one showcasing the finest innovative ideas and projects of their nation geared to addressing the critical global debates we face today.

On our journey through the Expo 2020 Dubai site we will discover several leading Italian companies that contributed to the development of the vast complex and assisted in the realization of the pavilions of many participating countries. All these contributions highlight again the Italian expertise and hallmark savoir faire, and also the important presence and cooperation between Italy, the UAE, and the world.

Expo 2020 Dubai closed on 31 March 2022. However, its legacy will remain in the form of a new district named "Expo City Dubai", a modern human-centric city created from 80% of the Expo site, and designed to offer "a model for innovative urban districts geared towards collaboration, knowledge-sharing and talent creation for the benefit of future generations".[1]

[1] "Expo City Dubai – the spirit of Expo 2020 Expo Dubai lives on" (22 June 2022), *Bureau International des Expositions*. https://www.bie-paris.org/site/en/news-announcements/expo-dubai-2020-2/expo-city-dubai-the-spirit-of-expo-2020-dubai-lives-on.

"Braiding the Future", an installation for Eni by Carlo Ratti and Italo Rota, presenting Eni's commitment to energy transition and decarbonization. The installation is a 20-metre long cascade of liana vines, recreating microalgae cultivation.

The Thematic Districts

Landscape Design: LAND
(Landscape Architecture Nature Development)

Client: Hopkins Architects for EX20,
Bureau International des Expositions

Location: Dubai, UAE

Period of execution: 2015–2020

Area: 66,215 sq.m

The three Thematic Districts at Expo were distinguished by the diverse geometry, colours, and vegetation that emphasize the uniqueness of each one, reflecting the three central themes.

Below: Sustainability District, 2021.

Opposite: Mobility District, 2021.

Following pages: View of Expo Dubai, Mobility District, 2021.

The words chosen for the Expo's three thematic districts, Mobility, Opportunity, and Sustainability, represent the driving principles leading towards the sustainable development of society, where citizens will find a closer relationship with nature. These guidelines are now important more than ever, considering the global phenomena we all face in these challenging times, which are leading to a change in everyday behaviours in our cities and the spaces we live and move in.

In this context, the landscape architect is summoned to be the mediator in the dialectic between built reality and cultivated nature, between economic needs and social demands, in a perspective of sustainability and solidarity that considers all its holistic components: environment, society, and economy.

Developing sustainable projects, working toward communities, leading sustainable development with nature-based solutions for a more performing urban nature with the aim to improve people's quality of life is the core of the landscape architecture firm LAND.

Since 2015 LAND had been closely involved in the Hopkins design masterplan of Expo 2020 Dubai, focusing on the deep roots people have with their surroundings and history, to create something intrinsic with the nature of this place.

Their commitment to Expo 2020 Dubai involved the vision and the design of the public realm for the Thematic Districts, where these sub-themes meet their principles

of best practice for sustainable development.
The Thematic Districts, the integral part of the Expo 2020 Dubai site, comprises 86 permanent buildings spread over three separate "petals".
LAND gave each of the three petals a unique character, portrayed through different geometry, landscaping, and colours to reflect the three main Expo 2020 Dubai themes.
Their approach consisted of the deep reading of the territory's roots, and for each theme, they identified an element of nature related to the UAE region landscape.
Water, permanently on the move, represented the Mobility District. As the driving force of all Nature, it is behind mankind's earliest mechanical inventions. Since the beginning of human history, water and the sea have been the primary connective means between civilizations. This is particularly true for the shores of the UAE, where people have met since ancient times, especially for trade purposes. Long before the oil industry began, this was the real soul of the UAE.
The desert, a sea of sand, defined the Opportunity District. Like ships on the water, trade caravans brought wealth and culture along their routes. However, the desert is also the place of mirages. It is up to us to make those visions real, and transform them into a viable programme for the future.
Last but not least is vegetation, associated with Sustainability. Trees and plants mitigate even the worst effects of human activities, contributing to a significant environmental balance. In the UAE landscape, vegetation finds an exceptionally welcoming environment in the Oasis. Its environmental character allows people to collaborate with Nature based on a mutual – almost balanced – alliance.
The Public Realm of the Thematic Districts is characterized by a series of tree-lined, self-shaded, human-scaled streets with various sized and themed courtyard spaces.
A central spine runs through each District, creating places with water features, event stages, activity areas, and inspiring rest places clustered underneath a series of multifaceted elegant structures providing shade. Off the central spine are a series of intimate streets that encouraged visitors to explore and discover new places and spaces.
As landscape architects, LAND works with nature constantly; hence the use of varied vegetation approaches was fundamental to emphasize the uniqueness of each District.
Along the main spine of the Mobility District are combined orchards, palm groves, the cultivation of spices, but also the more recently introduced ornamental trees.
These choices recalled the idea of exploration. Plants have been exported and imported; new species have changed the identity of the landscape with new uses and new knowledge. Instead, in the Opportunity District, the species on the central spine recreate the typical landscape of wadis, with the wadi fig as the defining tree.

Just one species of trees characterize all the secondary places around.
Planting in the Sustainability District showcases vegetation's incredible adaptability and growth in extreme and demanding arid environments. It also testifies to mankind's ability to live and make a living from these landscapes with brilliant and innovative solutions that can become an example for a more conscious future and sustainable resource management.
The central spine displays the landscape of rivers and floodplains. They are characterized by acacia trees and shrubs growing around rocks at the foot of the mound.
The secondary areas around celebrate the local flora.
Also carefully chosen was the materiality applied to each district, bearing in mind the properties of the region's harsh climate.
The proposed paving material is durable, hard-wearing, and consists of a light palette of natural stone and concrete paving.
The Landscape of "EXPO 2020 Dubai Thematic Districts" had been entirely designed in BIM (Building Information Modelling) using Autodesk Revit. The agronomic know-how, which LAND possesses, has been translated into a BIM language and imported into a set of parameters useful to design the three thematic districts and their public realms.
The project had been designed to achieve LEED Gold level. It is going to be repurposed in legacy mode to create a campus of buildings interconnected via bridge links that overlook landscaped areas, offering a district for innovative start-ups and tech companies.

Text by LAND and Lucia Pizzinato

Alif – The Mobility Pavilion

Company: Permasteelisa Group

Architecture Design: Foster + Partners

Client: EMAAR

Main Contractor: ALEC Engineering and Contracting LLC

Location: Dubai, UAE

Period of execution: 2018–2020

Area: 29,695 sq.m

Named after the first letter of the Arabic alphabet – *alif* – the Mobility Pavilion at Expo 2020 was one of the event's three signature pavilions. It was based on the sub-theme of Mobility: how people move, explore, and connect, aiming to provide opportunities for people to connect, collaborate and share knowledge to enable regional and global communities to develop for the future.
Designed by the renowned architectural studio Foster + Partners, the pavilion is located at the south entrance of the Expo site. The architecture, a striking tiered trefoil-shaped building, is inserted in a dynamic landscape conceived as a fairground with a high-speed undulating track in a loop around the pavilion and demonstration areas showing the latest technological innovations related to Mobility.
Expression of the dynamic nature of the building is the façade. The architectural envelope was realized by the International Permasteelisa Group. Its envelope features horizontal stainless steel fins which are double-curved, changing its

Mobility Pavilion characterized by the "trefoil shaped" building.

Opposite: Close-up of the Pavilion's glazed façade made by Permasteelisa Group.

cross-section as it moves towards the building core giving the pavillon façade a unique dynamic effect. These fins rise to form a canopy for each of the three entrances, self-shading the building and reflecting the heat, while the roof hosts an array of combined photovoltaic and solar hot-water panels.
Due to its challenging architectural shape, the Mobility Pavilion required a very innovative approach, as well as a good material understanding and knowledge.
The main complexity of the building was given by its conical shape as well as from the horizontal stainless-steel fins that have a variable geometry. To address the challenge of the envelope, special 3D software skills and a smart engineering approach were required as well as integrated BMU (Building Maintenance Unit) tracks for maintenance and cleaning of the façade and LED lighting fixtures for illuminating the pavilion..
Designed to LEED Gold standards, this is one of the pavilions that will become part of "Expo City Dubai".

Al Wasl Plaza Expo Dubai 2020

Company: Cimolai & RIMOND Middle East Contracting LLC

Architecture Design: Adrian Smith + Gordon Gill Architecture

Client: Expo 2020 Dubai

Location: Dubai, UAE

Period of execution: 2017–2020

Area: 724,000 sq.m

The centrepiece of the Expo 2020 Dubai was Al Wasl Plaza, a semi-open space connecting the three main "petals" of the Thematic Districts. Encircled by an intricate dome trellis designed by Adrian Smith and Gordon Gill, the plaza combines breathtaking design and innovative technology, incorporating a 360° immersive projection experience.

The Italian companies Cimolai and RIMOND were appointed in 2017 as the main contractor to deliver the complex masterpiece. The dome extending over 130 metres of the central area with a height of approximately 67 metres is an articulated structure of steel tubes organized in a pattern of interconnected rings varying in shape and size.

A complex lifting operation was conducted to position the prefabricated steel crown on the top of the trellis. The process required eighteen hydraulic jacks, aided by steel hauling cables attached to 18 freestanding temporary columns.

The internal part of the structure forms an enclosure with 632 transparent membranes serving as sunshades. This translucent surface of PTFE fabric also provides a screen for video projections, and comprises 2,800 LED show lights and 252 projectors.
After the Expo's six-month run, the plaza will continue to play a significant role at "Expo City Dubai", a central hub linking up the surrounding mixed-use buildings and the neighbouring districts.

At night, the majestic dome is transformed into a multimedia screen onto which colourful animated stories are projected, 2021.

Opposite: View of Al Wasl Plaza's dome, centrepiece of the Exposition, 2021.

Italian Pavillion

Italian Pavilion, Expo Dubai by Carlo Ratti & Italo Rota, 2021.

TA

Paolo Glisenti

General Commissioner of Italy at Expo 2020 Dubai

Italy's presence at Expo 2020 Dubai

Detail of the pavilion's walls made of nautical ropes produced with recycled plastic (ca. two million bottles). The intricate vertical meshwork stretches for almost 70 km in length.

Opposite: Starting point of the pavilion exhibition: the atomic clock of the Italian aerospace company Leonardo, serving as a metaphor of perfect time.

Italy's past contribution to the urban and industrial development of the United Arab Emirates has to a certain extent provided inspiration for the narrative architecture of the Italian Pavilion at Expo 2020 Dubai: a structure recounting the history of Italy constantly sailing in search of new lands, new minds, new cultures.

I would like to think that our Pavilion has succeeded in showing how the innovative solutions now required to face the challenges posed by the critical demand of real estate and the need for resilient production plants in the years ahead can be deeply connected to creativity. The Italian Pavilion intended to provide a demonstrative site of how urban and industrial development could become a global creative economy.

In this regard, Italy's Pavilion at Expo 2020 Dubai was imagined, designed, and built as a new carbon-free recyclable habitat made with compostable structural components, biological materials, and natural fittings currently in the marketplace as opportunities for developers, engineers, and entrepreneurs.

A Pavilion with natural air-conditioning and oxygenation, smart lighting systems, paint material made from food-waste, along with compostable walls and ceilings that set a new standard for future for energy-efficient, environmentally protective, and human safer housing and manufacturing. A regenerative design for a regenerating economy.

The legacy of Italy's participation in Expo 2020 Dubai is embodied in this strict connection between memory and innovation, between the past and the future, between traditionally admired Italian creativity and forward-looking Italian inventiveness and ingenuity.

Davide Rampello

Artistic Director of the Italian Pavillion at Expo 2020 Dubai

Beauty Connects People

View of the area dedicated to temporary exhibitions, on a rotation every 15 days.

Opposite: The round structure topped by a dome and covered with Mediterranean herbs evoking a Renaissance garden is the Belvedere (on the right). On the opposite side stands part the digital installation by Enel X, "Second Sun" and "Second Moon", which creates a crescendo of lighting effects through the changing colour temperature in the course of the day.

The theme of the Italian Pavilion at Expo Dubai 2020 was "La Bellezza unisce le Persone" (Beauty Connects People), a tribute to the etymology of the word *bellezza*, which harmonically conflates the concepts of beautiful, true, good, and just. The Latin root of *bellus*, diminutive of *bonus*, refers to the principles of order and proportion expressed in Greek philosophy, endorsing the intrinsic and indissoluble link between Italian culture and that enduring cradle of civilization – the Mediterranean – with its connections and intercultural and inter-religious dialogue.

As an ever-present agent, *bellezza* deftly conflates the know-how and multidisciplinary aptitudes of past, present, and future. It unites and interlaces the principles of style, cultural and spiritual knowledge, project-oriented skills and creative genius, combining tradition and innovation. As a connector of human histories and geographies, *bellezza* offers a unique narrative, a dramatic and emotive itinerary interweaving creative inspiration and research.

The exhibition offered a narrative of creativity, research, and multidisciplinary planning, dovetailing the distinct branches of manufacturing and technology, scientific processes, education and training, art and culture. It demonstrated how art and science are mutually inclusive passions, a braiding of seemingly distant worlds.

Italy Pavilion

Architecture Design: CRA-Carlo Ratti Associati and Italo Rota Building Office, with matteogatto&associati and F&M Ingegneria

Companies: Fincantieri, Mapei, Gruppo Boero

Project Management Consultant: LC&Partners Project Management and Engineering

Client: Commissioner for Italy's participation at Expo 2020 Dubai

Location: Dubai, UAE

Period of execution: 2019–2021

Area: 3,500 sq.m

The Italian Pavilion at Expo Dubai 2020, designed by CRA-Carlo Ratti Associati and Italo Rota Building Office with Matteo Gatto and F&M Ingegneria, proposes an all-encompassing vision of "circular" architecture: a multimedia façade composed of two million recycled plastic bottles replaces all perimeter walls and invites the visitor to explore an entirely new world of building materials – from algae and coffee-grounds to orange-peel and sand. Instead of air-conditioning, a localized cooling system integrated with intermittent "misting" provide extensive shading, natural ventilation, and optimal thermal comfort.

The pavilion is an embodiment of the principles of reuse and recycling. Designed and constructed by Fincantieri – Europe's largest shipwright – the building's roof comprises three "hulls" that will continue their journey after Expo. These three hulls vary in length from 40 to 50 metres, and are supported by more than 150 slender steel pillars, which express how architecture is able to transform itself, and challenges the standard way buildings are developed for temporary events – such as world Expos – whereby many purpose-built structures end up in landfills after just a few months of life. Seen from above, the green white and red

Views to and from the suspended skywalk, which leads visitors on a trail of discovery through the pavilion's installations, such as the LED reproduction of the Fibonacci sequence by Mario Merz on the left.

3
21
34
55
89
144
233

hulls of the building are coated with an innovative paint produced by Gruppo Boero, and form what has already been dubbed as the largest ever example of Italy's "Tricolore" national flag, covering some 2,100 sq.m.
Visitors enter the Italian Pavilion via an escalator that conveys them to a walkway suspended 11 metres above ground. From this floating vantage point they could observe all the exhibits and installations at once, then descend to view them close-up. In this way, Italy's contributions to the Expo offered an echo of the nineteenth-century "Grand Tour" that saw enchanted Europeans travelling through France and Italy.
The building materials for the exhibits and the structure itself adopt the aforementioned "circular" approach of renewables and recycling, developed in collaboration with the Milan-based company Mapei, which manufactures chemical products for the construction industry. The pavilion itself rests on a purpose-built dune five metres above ground-level made of locally sourced sand.
Visited by over 1.6 million people, the building won multiple accolades, from the Construction Innovation Awards, to the Exhibitors Award, and the Official Partecipants Award. Moreover, it has been featured among the highlights of Expo Dubai 2020 by international design media outlets, from CNN, to Fast Company, to *Wallpaper*, *Elle Decor*, *Dezeen* and *Interni*. The *New York Times* called it a "dazzling, over-scaled structure" among the "extraordinary architectural achievements" of Expo 2020, the first event of its kind to be held in the Arab world.

Text by Carlo Ratti and Italo Rota

View from above of the Spirulina Algae cultivation plant by the renewable energy company TOLO Green.

Opposite: Visitors entering the Italian Pavilion. The interior route starts via an escalator that takes patrons up to a skywalk suspended 11 metres above ground-level.

UAE Pavilion

Companies: Duplomatic Motion Solutions; Duplomatic Middle East Electromechanical Equipment Installation and Maintenance LLC (Roof Wing Opening System), Premier Composite Tecnologies (composite materials)

Lead/Principal Architect, Lead Principal Engineer: Santiago Calatrava

Client: UAE Ministry of Presidential Affairs

Main Contractor: Arabtec Construction LLC; ALEC Engineering and Contracting LLC

Location: Al Forsan, Al Wasl Plaza, Dubai, UAE

Period of execution: 2017–2021

Area: 20,900 sq.m

The United Arab Emirates Pavilion was a key attraction ensconced in the Expo's Opportunity District, facing the Al Wasl Plaza. Designed by the world-renowned architect Santiago Calatrava, the pavilion was conceived to "evoke the pioneering spirit and power of connections that transformed the UAE from a collection of small, desert communities, into a global connection point."[1]
The building's alluring form evokes a falcon in flight, symbol of the UAE's culture and heritage, and represents an outstanding combination of art and engineering. The entire structure is effectively a complex machine whose architecture is characterized by the stunning design of the roof, with its "falcon wings" composed of twenty-eight individual carbon-fibre elements that open and close. These mobile structures allow daylight to reach the photovoltaic cells integrated into the roof's design, thus generating clean energy for the operation of the building. During the night, the wings operate in conjunction with striking light effects providing an immersive experience for visitors.

Thanks to the technology engineered by Duplomatic Motion Solutions, the wings can be opened and closed during the day allowing the exposure of the solar panels installed on the roof of the building.

The company responsible for the roof wing opening system is the Italian firm Duplomatic, an internationally renowned high-technology company specializing in hydraulics and motion solutions, which in 2018 was commissioned for the design, manufacturing, installation, testing, and for the hydraulic system responsible for the movement of all the twenty-eight moving elements of the building's roof.
One of the most challenging aspects of the project was ensuring the synchronized movement of the structure in order to convey a sense of precision and rhythmic harmony, which is reinforced by the clean lines of the architectural design and the chromatic values of all the parts involved.
The technical solutions included the exacting choice of the main hydraulic parts, controlling the operating system pressure and flow-rate, the design of the electronics, and the related motion control algorithms to ensure a progressive and silent movement.
The result is a complex engineering "machine" that merges seamlessly with the building, comprising a power unit of 1MW installed in the pavilion's basement. Five separate hydraulic pumping systems, 2 kilometres of high-pressure pipes pumping up to 2,200 litres per minute of oil to the building's roof, where the forty-six hydraulic cylinders positioned under the wings ensure the synchronized movement of all the twenty-eight elements. This movement is choreographed by nine separate computers that automatically drive more than 2,000 points distributed across the entire building, including valves of different types and sensors, all connected with over 25 km of cabling.

Text by Paolo Leutenegger
and Lucia Pizzinato

[1] Quote by Reem Ebrahim Al Hashimy, Minister of State for International Cooperation and General Director of Expo 2020 Dubai. www.calatrava.com (accessed on 1 October 2021).

Pavilion Entrance, 2021, with the 28 "petal" elements fully open, covering a rotation range up to125 degrees.

Other contributions

Lucia Pizzinato

It is worth mentioning other significant contributions by the Italian expertise in the Expo Dubai 2020 site.

RIMOND was involved in the construction of other pavilions, including those for New Zealand, Finland, Spain, and Bahrain. They also delivered the "Casa Agusta", a helicopter terminal proposed by Leonardo, Italy's largest helicopter manufacturer. Designed by the Italian firm Archea Associati, "Casa Agusta" combines a helipad, a showroom, and lounge areas, in a single city-based heliport. The project supports the development of a network of point-to-point connections for both urban transfers to Expo Dubai 2020 and links between cities. It represents the essence of Italian design and technology, and the next step towards a newer and more sustainable form of mobility.

LC&Partners Project Management and Engineering followed the construction project management of eleven pavilions in addition to that of Italy, including those of the Netherlands, Latvia, Sweden, to name just a few.

Matteogatto&associati and its partners were called by Expo 2020 Dubai to assist 39 countries – part of the Thematic Districts – in the creation of the exhibition content and design.

Other interventions were also related to implementing the infrastructure system on the occasion of the grand event.

In 2017 RTA announced a 15-kilometre extension of Dubai's metro Red Line, known as Route 2020. This new tract of 3.2 km of underground rail, plus 11.8 km of the elevated line connects the Expo area with the heart of the city. The project Route 2020 comprised six stations, and featured an interchange hub on the Red Line.

Swissboring (Trevi Group) accomplished more than 50% of the piling and shoring works for the metro rail, and solely did the piling works for the iconic main station for Expo 2020 Dubai.

Prysmian Group provided the entire underground power and communication system cables to cover all functionalities with the latest cable design solutions in terms of chemical and mechanical resistance, fire resistance, and enhanced transmission capacity.

Confirmed again was Rizzani de Eccher, which was selected to build all 11.8 km of the elevated guideway, while the company's engineering team was engaged in the structural design of the viaduct superstructure.

An active participant in the development of the Expo site was also Mapei. Its products were chosen by several pavilions, thanks to the company's high quality and sustainability properties and its ability to meet all the different designers' requirements. Morocco, Australia, Brazil, Al Wasl Plaza and the Thematic Districts are among the many works the firm carried out.

Furthermore, Mapei was involved in the excavation work of the metro line supplying the products for underground works to the Expo Link consortium. In addition, it contributed to the building of roads and bridges for Route 2020.[1]

Along the main causeway and roundabout that leads to the Expo site lies a special decorative feature of urban beautification devised by the Italian company 3FI, whose unique patented system "Afffresco" combines the modern art of digital photography with the ancient fresco technique to embed a digital image into almost any surface, which lasts for a lifetime. The company's creations grace many of the tunnels, bridges, ramps, and underpasses of Dubai and Abu Dhabi.

On the occasion of the Expo, RTA commissioned the company 30,000 sq.m of decoration in 2019. Parsons provided in part the design, and the work was completed in 2020. An extension of another 5,000 sq.m of Afffresco was added at the beginning of 2021. The pattern clearly shows such a marble design with some embedded 3D-effect Expo logos, definitely an amazing solution compared to the otherwise bland grey concrete surface.

All these Italian companies contributed actively to Expo 2020 Dubai, leaving a legacy, thanks to their vision for the future and their commitment toward innovative sustainability as essential values of their operational philosophy.

[1] "Leading by Example" (Digital Issue n. 185, October 2021), Big Project ME, wwwMEConstructionNews.com https://meconstructionnews.com/emagazine/tbp_preview.php? issue=185&code=big_project_oct_2021&m=10&y=2021. pp. 10-11.

Decoration by 3F fro Expo Dubai. The gold ring, the symbol of the Exposition, is applied tridimensionally on the columns' road that brings to the Expo Site 2021.

“Modern” Afffresco is applied along the wall of the main road towards the Expo site.

List of Contacts

This list provides each company's general information and contacts through their representative website, and current office address in Italy and in the United Arab Emirates.

Following pages: The Dubai skyline seen from Al Satwa, 2015, and view from Al Maryah Island, Abu Dhabi, 2017.

Architecture and Engineering

ACPV ARCHITECTS Antonio Citterio Patricia Viel
Milan, Italy
www.citterio-viel.com

BMS Progetti S.r.l.
Milan, Italy
www.bmsprogetti.it

CRA Carlo Ratti Associati
Turin, Italy
www.carloratti.com

Cotefa.ingegneri&architetti
Brescia and Pavia, Italy
Abu Dhabi, United Arab Emirates
www.cotefa.com

De8_Architetti
Orio al Serio (Bergamo) and Crema, Italy
www.deottostudio.com

F&M Ingegneria S.p.A.
Mirano (Venice), Milan, Rome, Italy
F&M Retail
Dubai, United Arab Emirates
www.fm-ingegneria.com

General Planning S.r.l.
Milan, Italy
www.generalplanning.com

iBridge Engineering Consultancy LLC
Abu Dhabi, United Arab Emirates
www.becuae.com

ItalMesh S.r.l.
Montirone (Brescia), Italy
Dubai, United Arab Emirates
www.italmesh.com

Italo Rota Building Office
Milan, Italy

LAND Landscape Architecture Nature Development S.r.l.
Milan, Italia
www.landsrl.com

matteogatto&ssociati
Milan, Italy
www.matteogatto.com

MMA Projects S.r.l.
Barlassina (Milano), Italy
www.mmaprojects.com

M+N Architecture S.r.l.
Florence, Italy
Abu Dhabi, United Arab Emirates
www.mn-architecture.com

Nesite S.p.A.
Padua, Italy
Hamriyah, Sharjah
www.nesite.com

Progetto MCK S.r.l.
Monza, Italy
abambini@progettomck.it

Sgaravatti Group
Capoterra (Cagliari), Italy
Dubai, United Arab Emirates
www.sgaravattigroup.it
www.muchmore.ae

SPATIUM
Milan, Italy
www.spatium.it

Studio Costa Architecture
Rome, Italy
Dubai, United Arab Emirates
www.studiocosta.ae

Studio Valle Progettazioni
Rome, Italy
www.studiovalle.com

Systematica S.r.l.
Milan, Italy
www.systematica.net

Urbanism Planning Architecture UPA Italia S.r.l.
Milan, Italy
www.upaitalia.com
UPA Consultancy LLC
Abu Dhabi, United Arab Emirates
www.upa.ae

Whitespace Architects
Amsterdam, Netherlands
Dubai, United Arab Emirates
www.whitespace.ae

Construction and Engineering

Cimolai S.p.A.
Porcia (Pordenone), Italy
www.cimolai.com

Danieli & C. Officine Meccaniche S.p.A.
Buttrio (Udine), Italy
Abu Dhabi, United Arab Emirates
www.danieli.com

Duplomatic Motion Solutions S.p.A.
Parabiago (Milan), Italy
Duplomatic Middle East Electromechanical Equipment Installation and Maintenance LLC
Dubai, United Arab Emirates
www.duplomaticsolutions.com

FEAL S.p.A.
Milan, Italy
It does not exist anymore

Maeg Costruzioni S.p.A.
Vazzola (Treviso), Italy
www.maegspa.com

MAPEI S.p.A.
Milan, Italy
www.mapei.com
MAPEI CONSTRUCTION CHEMICALS LLC
Dubai, United Arab Emirates
www.mapei.ae

Metra S.p.A.
Rodengo Saiano (Brescia), Italy
www.metra.eu

Permasteelisa Group
Vittorio Veneto, Italy
Dubai, United Arab Emirates
www.permasteelisagroup.com

Prysmian Group
Milan, Italy
Dubai, United Arab Emirates
www.prysmiangroup.com

REDAELLI TECNA S.p.A.
Cologno Monzese (Milan), Italy
www.teufelberger-redaelli.com

RIMOND S.r.l.
Milan, Italy
RIMOND Middle East General Contracting LLC
Abu Dhabi, United Arab Emirates
www.rimond.com

Rizzani de Eccher S.p.A.
Pozzuolo del Friuli (Udine), Italy
Dubai, United Arab Emirates
www.rizzanideeccher.com

Salini Impregilo (now Webuild S.p.A.)
Milan and Rome, Italy
Abu Dhabi and Dubai, United Arab Emirates
www.webuildgroup.com

Studio Geotecnico Nesti / Italengineering Middle East
Dubai, United Arab Emirates
Ras Al Khaimah, United Arab Emirates
www.nesti.it
www.italengineering-middle-east.com

Swissboring Overseas Piling Corporation LLC (Trevi Group)
Cesena, Italy
Abu Dhabi and Dubai, United Arab Emirates
www.swissboring.com
www.trevigroup.com

Design

Artemide S.p.A.
Pregnana Milanese (Milan), Italy
Artemide Middle East
d3 Dubai, United Arab Emirates
www.artemide.com

Fantini Mosaici S.r.l.
Milan, Italy
Abu Dhabi, United Arab Emirates
www.fantinimosaici.it

Poltrona Frau S.p.A.
Tolentino (Macerata), Italy
www.poltronafrau.com

3FI S.r.l.
Rome, Italy
www.afffresco.com

Energy Sector

Ansaldo Energia S.p.A.
Genoa, Italy
Abu Dhabi, United Arab Emirates
www.ansaldoenergia.com

Fisia Italimpianti S.p.A. (Webuild Group)
Genoa, Italy
Abu Dhabi, United Arab Emirates
www.fisiait.com

Maire Tecnimont S.p.A.
Milan, Italy
Abu Dhabi, United Arab Emirates
www.mairetecnimont.com

Saipem S.p.A.
San Donato Milanese (Milan), Italy
Abu Dhabi, Dubai, Sharjah, United Arab Emirates
www.saipem.com

Techint Engineering & Construction
Milan, Italy
www.techint.com

Tenaris
Dalmine (Bergamo), Italy
Dubai and Abu Dhabi, United Arab Emirates
www.tenaris.com

Marble, Stone, Porcelain and Slab Manufacturers

Atlas Concorde S.p.A.
Spezzano di Fiorano (Modena), Italy
Dubai, United Arab Emirates
www.atlasconcorde.com

GranitiFiandre S.p.A.
Castellarano (Reggio Emilia), Italy
www.granitifiandre.com

Henraux S.p.A.
Querceta (Lucca), Italy
www.henraux.it

LAMINAM S.p.A.
Fiorano Modenese (Modena), Italy
www.laminam.com

LASA MARMO S.r.l.
Lasa (Bolzano) and Verona, Italy
www.lasamarmo.it

Savema S.p.A.
Pietrasanta (Lucca), Italy
www.savema.com

Tre Emme / Landi Group S.r.l.
Seravezza (Lucca), Italy
www.landimarble.com

Project Management and Real Estate Development

LC&Partners Project Management and Engineering S.r.l.
Milan, Italy
Dubai, United Arab Emirates
www.lcandpartners.com

Preatoni Real Estate Development LLC
Dubai, United Arab Emirates
www.preatoni.net

Photo Credits

© Chris Goldstraw: pp. 114–115
© Marc Goodwin: pp. 158, 159, 160–161, 162, 163
© Michele Nastasi: cover, pp. 20–21, 48–49, 60, 61, 62, 63, 64–65, 66, 67, 186–187, 188–189
© Michele Nastasi. Courtesy of CRA-Carlo Ratti Associati and Italo Rota: pp. 14–15, 156, 166–167, 168, 169, 170, 171, 172, 173, 174, 175
© Shutterstock: pp. 54–55
Courtesy of 3FI: pp. 181, 182–183
Courtesy of Ansaldo Energia: pp. 150, 151
Courtesy of Andrea Bambini: pp. 42, 43
Courtesy of Cimolai: pp. 72, 73
Courtesy of Danieli & C. Officine Meccaniche: pp. 138–139, 139
Courtesy of ItalMesh: pp. 124–125
Courtesy of Laminam: pp. 122, 122–123
Courtesy of Maeg Costruzioni: pp. 86, 87, 88–89
Courtesy of Mapei: p. 57 top
Courtesy of Maire Tecnimont: pp. 136–137, 142–143
Courtesy of Preatoni Real Estate Development: p. 113
Courtesy of Rizzani de Eccher Archive: pp. 44, 45
Courtesy of Saipem: pp. 144–145, 145, 148, 149
Courtesy of Sgaravatti Group: pp. 40, 41
Courtesy of Studio Costa Architecture pp. 116, 117
Courtesy of Studio Valle Progettazioni: pp. 46–47
Courtesy of Techint: pp. 146–147
Courtesy of Tenaris: pp. 152–153
Courtesy of Webuild: pp. 4(detail), 58–59, 74, 75
Courtesy of Whitespace Architects: pp. 120, 121
Barbara Burg & Oliver Schuh, Palladium Photodesign: pp. 176–177, 178–179
Celso Creer II. Courtesy of UPA: pp. 76, 77, 78–79
© Duncan Chard. Courtesy of Fantini Mosaici: pp. 50, 51, 52, 53
© Luca Casonato. Courtesy of Rizzani de Eccher: p. 56, 57 bottom
Louvre Abu Dhabi @ Roland Halbe: pp.98, 99, 100, 101
© Pietro Facendola, Giulio Asso (Verdekiwi Photography). Courtesy of M+N Architecture: pp. 82, 83, 84, 84–85
Amedeo Gambino: pp. 130–131, 131
Paolo Marzi. Courtesy of SPATIUM: pp. 68, 69, 70, 70–71
© Edoardo Montaina. Courtesy Fisia Italimpianti: pp. 140, 141
© Edoardo Montaina. Courtesy of Webuild: pp. 132–133, 133
© Pino Musi. Courtesy of Fantini Mosaici: pp. 90, 91, 92, 93, 94, 95, 96, 97
© Tushar Naik. Courtesy of MMA Projects: pp. 106, 107
© Lucia Pizzinato: pp. 110, 111
© Leo Torri. Courtesy of ACPV ARCHITECTS Antonio Citterio Patricia Viel: pp. 102, 103, 104–105, 105
© Christophe Viseux. Courtesy of RIMOND: pp. 164, 165
© Jon Wallis Photography. Courtesy of UPA: pp. 80–81
© Jon Wallis Photography: pp. 108–109
© Nigel Young / Foster + Partners. Courtesy of RIMOND: pp. 118, 119
Lorenzo Zoli: pp. 126–127, 128–129, 129